REFRESHED BY THE WORD

CYCLE A

by
John E. O'Brien

PAULIST PRESS
New York/Mahwah

Cover design by James F. Brisson

Nihil Obstat: Rev. James M. Cafone, S.T.D., *Censor Librorum*
Imprimatur: Most Rev. Theodore E. McCarrick, D.D., Archbishop of Newark

Library of Congress Cataloging-in-Publication Data

O'Brien, John E., 1921-
    Refreshed by the Word : cycle A / by John E. O'Brien.
        p.   cm.
    ISBN 0-8091-3597-3 (paper).
    1. Church year meditations.   2. Prayer groups—Catholic Church.   3. Catholic Church—Custom and practices. 4. Common lectionary—Meditations. I. Title.
BX2170.C55O32 1994   94-20569
263'.9—dc20   CIP

Published by Paulist Press
997 Macarthur Boulevard
Mahwah, NJ 07430

Printed and bound in the
United States of America

Contents

Acknowledgments

Refreshed by the Word is a communal work. I wish to acknowledge and thank the following people who are part of its history.

Msgr. Tom Kleissler, who invited me to write my reflections on the Sunday readings and whose critical insights have helped to sharpen their focus.

Mary C. McGuinness, O.P. and Rev. John Russell, for their helpful critiquing and editing.

International Office of RENEW staff members and volunteers, for writing creative prayers that can be used to open the sessions.

Sr. Joan Marie Ricca, S.S.J. and Eileen Brown, for their help with scripture quotations.

Julie Jones, for her typing and research help in preparing the manuscript.

Small Christian community members from the Archdioceses of Newark and Hartford, who piloted various sections and offered valuable comments.

Maria Maggi, editor at Paulist Press, for her encouragement and suggestions.

*Dedicated to Betty O'Brien and Bridie Watson
for continued encouragement and support*

Foreword

Father John O'Brien has made a real contribution with this book. Often we rush to the latest, most innovative program for adult religious education. The fact is that the church's real textbook is the Bible, specifically the three cycles of the lectionary. How rich the liturgy of the word would become, if folks encountered the word either before or after it is proclaimed in church liturgically. Father O'Brien's materials can be used in a variety of ways—by those in intentional small communities, or by any parish group or ministering group seeking to gain a more communal foundation for their activity. The book could also be used by families. Thus, the book makes possible an experience of church not frequently enough had by many Catholics: not only the large assembly, but also church as small group or community, and the domestic church of family.

In Father O'Brien's simple materials, we have the essence of small group experience as well as androgogy at its best: people gathered around God's word, in prayer, sharing their lives with each other, and moving out in action to transform the world.

This book will be of great assistance to groups/communities in the post-RENEW era, as well as for those ministerial, seasonal and small Christian communities who are already making an impact on the church of the future. It is a welcome addition to our collection of pastoral tools.

Patrick J. Brennan
President, National Center
for Evangelization and
Parish Renewal

Introduction

A new energy in parish life is emerging throughout the world. Small communities and faith-sharing are becoming a more normative part of the very fabric of parish life. This is occurring in a variety of ways. People are gathering in small groups during different seasons of the year to pray, share faith and support one another; people in similar ministries are praying together and sharing faith during their meeting times, thus supporting one another both in their lives and in their ministries; and significant numbers of people are making a commitment to pray and share with others in small communities in an ongoing way, allowing the gospel to touch every aspect of their lives.

Refreshed by the Word, Cycle A, offers refreshing, lively insights into the word of God. Using the Sunday lectionary readings of Cycle A as a starting point, prayers, reflections, provocative faith questions are proposed that are applicable to every parishioner, every Christian who desires to grow in the life of God. (Note that the presentation of materials follows the same sequence as the Sunday readings of the lectionary.)

Refreshed by the Word, Cycle A can be utilized in a variety of ways. First, the members of parish committees, organizations and ministries can enhance their time as they gather for their regular meetings. For example, when parishioners on a pastoral council or finance council meet they could use these materials to pray and reflect together and better internalize the values of Jesus in their ministry. Using these materials on a regular basis would insure that all parish meetings become more spiritually based. Instead of lengthening meetings these materials would provide a spiritual enrichment which could focus meetings, help decisions to be made more readily and, in fact, may even shorten many long-drawn-out meetings.

Second, the materials are also designed in such a way that they can be used by seasonal small groups who gather to share their life and faith at various times during the year. Many parishioners like the concept of meeting seasonally, for example, during Lent and during the autumn. The materials are designed so that people can enter into the process of prayer and faith sharing at any time of the year and be comfortable with the word and the process. And because parishes always have some new parishioners who have not had the experience of being in a small Christian community, inviting parishioners to be part of a seasonal small group gives them a taste of what a small Christian community is about.

Third, the materials offer ample information for parishioners who are entering into or are already involved in small Christian communities. They can be used whether people meet weekly, every other week or monthly.

PROCESS

Each group using *Refreshed by the Word* needs to have a small group/community leader or facilitator who is familiar with both the materials and the process. In addition, the leader should check the Ordo or church calendar to ensure that the proper Sunday readings are used. Because the time of Lent and Easter is movable, the Sundays in Ordinary Time are not static either and it would be well for the leader to check the Ordo.

The materials are designed in such a way that the process could take as long as an hour-and a-half or be as short as twenty minutes. If a seasonal small group or a small Christian community is meeting primarily for prayer and faith sharing, they would use all the components; if a committee or ministerial community is meeting, the participants may wish to read only one or two readings, the reflection, and share briefly on one or two of the sharing questions. If two are selected, the first and third would be most appropriate since they are connected by the same theme.

In order to assist the leader, a missal or missalette which includes the alternative opening prayer for Sunday and the responsorial psalm would be helpful. These can be procured in a number of ways. If the parish has a subscription service, they can order extra copies for small group use or leaders can borrow from the church supply. Often individuals subscribe to a service themselves and can share their copies for the time of meeting.

Leaders are also encouraged to be creative in preparing an appropriate setting for prayer and sharing and to eliminate as far as possible any distractions.

Weekly Outline

OPENING PRAYER

Each session may begin with a time of focusing on the presence of God through quiet reflection or soft music. The leader may use the alternate opening prayer of the Sunday liturgy, prepare another brief prayer, invite another participant to pray, or choose an appropriate prayer from the Prayer Resources.

GREETINGS AND ACTION RESPONSE SHARING

At the first session or whenever there is a new participant, all are invited to introduce themselves and, perhaps, share something about themselves.

At other sessions, this time is used to share with others about experiences that resulted from the previous week's Action Response segment.

LISTENING AND SHARING THE WORD

Each person reads the scripture silently.

Ideally each participant will have already reflected on the background and the scripture prior to the session. However, it may be helpful to read the background again aloud with a few moments of silence.

Follow with a short prayer invoking the Holy Spirit.

The scripture is then proclaimed aloud followed by a suitable time of silent prayer.

Each person then shares his/her response to the scripture. The questions may provide a good guide. The focus is on how one experiences the action of God in his/her life and what that means in daily life.

ACTION RESPONSE

The leader will help the group focus on specific action responses that could flow from the week's sharing. Each person could choose an individual action or the group as a whole could choose a common action to undertake. (Suggested Action Responses are included in a separate listing after the Prayer Resource section.) Ministerial communities may simply decide that their tasks at hand will be their response. However, the task at hand need not necessarily be their only response. The word of God always challenges us anew. It is helpful to invite participants to share their commitments. At the beginning of the next session the leader would open with prayer and then invite people to volunteer to share how they carried out their action responses. In this way a gentle form of accountability is used to help people concretely realize how they are living out the word, how they are being "good news" for others.

PRAYER

The gathering is concluded with some time for prayer. The leader may wish to ask someone to be responsible for leading the closing prayer. Suggested closing prayers are given; however, the leader or participants may wish to select their own or close with spontaneous prayer.

REMINDER

Any announcements can be made in preparation for the upcoming week or season.

SMALL GROUP/COMMUNITY FAITH SHARING

Small group/community sessions are a very important part of the parish's spiritual growth and development process. These small group-ings provide a rare opportunity for us, the people of God, to share our faith, to listen more closely to the Spirit, and to witness that God has called us, touched us and healed us as individuals, families, neighbors and parishioners.

Understanding and respecting the ways adults learn is an essential part of small faith sharing groups. It is important that the atmosphere be comfortable, warm and friendly. Ambiguity and difference of opinion need to be expected. Each person is given the opportunity to express feelings and thoughts, examined in light of the rich scriptural tradition of our faith. Being accepted and listened to are essential ingredients of a good faith sharing experience. There should be a true desire to listen to another's experience. A sense of humor is always helpful!

The leader/facilitator is the person who has responsibility for guiding the group through the faith sharing and prayers (or assigning it to one of the members) of the small group session. Leaders of the small groups must be well trained for the task. By demonstrating charity and flexibility, a facilitator can effectively help the group to stay on the topic, gently include hesitant members and develop a warm, accepting, open climate and group cohesiveness.

Leaders do not provide preambles or prologues to questions; they do not frighten, shame or argue with participants by word, gesture, expression, voice tone or note taking. Participants may have questions about specific elements of our faith. Rather than trying to answer all questions, the facilitator may refer to the questions beyond the group resources to gain answers about our faith.

A leader listens carefully to the participants and asks questions only when necessary to keep the discussion moving or keep it on focus. The leader needs to be prepared by understanding beforehand the "questions" and the "background" provided in the text. However, the leader need never be a slave to a set of questions or text, but should be able to adapt to what is needed for the sharing as it moves along.

When two or more Christians share our faith, we are assured that Christ is in our midst and that the life of God and gifts of the Spirit are at work in us. Through the small group/community sessions we are in a very vital way opening ourselves to the Spirit's working in us and through us.

Faith Sharing Principles

In an effort to keep your group/community consistent with its purpose, we offer the following Faith Sharing Principles:

THEOLOGICAL PRINCIPLES

- EACH PERSON IS LED BY GOD ON HIS/HER PERSONAL SPIRITUAL JOURNEY. THIS HAPPENS IN THE CONTEXT OF THE CHURCH.

- FAITH SHARING REFERS TO SHARED REFLECTIONS ON THE ACTION OF GOD IN ONE'S LIFE EXPERIENCE as related to scripture and the church's faith. Faith sharing is not necessarily discussion, problem solving, or scripture study. The purpose is an encounter between a person in the concrete circumstances of one's life and the word of God which leads to a conversion of heart.

- FAITH SHARING IS MEANT TO SERVE OUR UNION WITH CHRIST AND HIS CHURCH AND THEREBY WITH ONE ANOTHER. With the help of God's Spirit we contribute vitality to the whole church. From the church we receive authoritative guidance from episcopal and priestly leadership. We are nurtured in the sacramental life. We are supported with a community of believers for our mission in the world.

- THE ENTIRE FAITH SHARING PROCESS IS SEEN AS PRAYER, i.e., listening to the word of God as broken open by others' experience.

SMALL GROUP GUIDELINES:

- CONSTANT ATTENTION TO RESPECT, HONESTY AND OPENNESS FOR EACH PERSON WILL ASSIST THE GROUP OR COMMUNITY'S GROWTH.

- EACH PERSON SHARES ON THE LEVEL WHERE HE/SHE FEELS COMFORTABLE.

- SILENCE IS A VITAL PART OF THE TOTAL PROCESS OF FAITH SHARING. Participants are given time to reflect before any sharing begins, and a period of comfortable silence might occur between individual sharings.

- PERSONS ARE ENCOURAGED TO WAIT TO SHARE A SECOND TIME UNTIL OTHERS WHO WISH TO DO SO HAVE CONTRIBUTED.

- THE ENTIRE GROUP IS RESPONSIBLE FOR PARTICIPATING AND FAITH SHARING.

- CONFIDENTIALITY IS ESSENTIAL, ALLOWING EACH PERSON TO SHARE HONESTLY.

- REACHING BEYOND THE GROUP IN ACTION AND RESPONSE IS ESSENTIAL FOR THE GROWTH OF INDIVIDUALS, THE GROUPS AND THE CHURCH.

ADVENT SEASON

First Sunday of Advent

OPENING PRAYER

The Alternate Opening Prayer of Today's Liturgy

READINGS: Isaiah 2:1–5; Romans 13:11–14a; Matthew 24:37–44.

REFLECTION

Advent is with us again. But Advent is more than a liturgical season of four weeks. It accents what is a constant in our lives beyond all seasons: the advent of God. The Lord comes in our daily journey and prayer, word, action and interaction with one another. We prepare for that coming now, for the coming in our individual deaths, and in the final coming at end time.

The scriptures focus on certain features of God's advent in time and in history. Isaiah stresses that the invitation is from the Lord, but that we must respond. "Come, let us climb the Lord's mountain." And again, "O House of Jacob, come, let us walk in the light of the Lord!"

Paul tells us to wake up from our slumber, and "throw off the works of darkness [and] put on the armor of light." This is our response to the urgent invitation in God's advent. Finally, Matthew accents the uncertainty of the Lord's advent: "For at an hour you do not expect, the Son of Man will come."

SHARING

How have I experienced any advent of God in our small group/ community interaction? Or if this is the first-time meeting, how do I expect to experience the advent of God?

What action can we point to this year when we have helped to turn "swords into plowshares" in the parish?

How does Paul's example of deeds of darkness—"rivalry and jealousy"—find any place in our group/community relationship?

During the Advent season what concrete action will I take to recognize the constant advent of God in my journey?

ACTION RESPONSE

Choose an action that will enable individuals or the group as a whole to live out in the coming week what has been shared.

PRAYER

Allow time for spontaneous prayer and conclude with praying the responsorial psalm of Sunday's liturgy, Psalm 122.

Second Sunday of Advent

OPENING PRAYER

The Alternative Opening Prayer of Today's Liturgy

READINGS: Isaiah 11:1–10; Romans 15:4–9; Matthew 3:1–12.

REFLECTION

The prophet of Advent, John the Baptist, comes out of the wilderness announcing that the advent of the reign of God is at hand. There is no doubt of his connecting with Isaiah as he uses his very words and imagery. "Prepare the way of the Lord, make straight God's paths." John makes the Isaiah symbol a reality, for "with the breath of his lips he shall slay the wicked." And who are the "wicked"? The unrepentant and indifferent Jew then, and the Christian now. He is speaking to no outside group but to insiders—to you and to me. We are the "brood of vipers." No more than the Jews can we claim special privilege, saying, "We have Abraham as our father." John means us when he answers, "God can raise up children to Abraham from these very stones."

And there is more. When the messiah advents, he will baptize with more than water. It shall be the cleansing, searing baptism of "the Holy Spirit and fire." Those of us, or that part of my life, which is unreformed and unjust will be like dead trees cut down and cast into the fire. The messiah means business. Jesus will gather all the grain of my life into God's barn but its chaff will be burned.

The Advent gospel of John mutes all cash registers and jingle bells and rings out loud and clear: "Reform your lives." Before the advent of God's justice and peace there must be a radical reformation within my way of living.

SHARING

What is peace? What is harmony? If our group disagrees over some questions, does that mean there is no peace?

Do we find "hope from the words of scripture"? (Romans) Give a concrete example from today's readings of a word or phrase which gives me hope.

"Reform your lives." What do I think that demands from me as an individual and as a member of this group/community?

What action will I take this week to reform my life?

ACTION RESPONSE

Choose an action that will enable individuals or the group as a whole to live out in the coming week what has been shared.

PRAYER

Allow time for spontaneous prayer and conclude with praying the responsorial psalm of Sunday's liturgy, Psalm 72.

Third Sunday of Advent

OPENING PRAYER

The Alternative Opening Prayer of Today's Liturgy

READINGS: Isaiah 35:1–6a, 10; James 5:7–10;
Matthew 11:2–11.

REFLECTION

The liturgy of the third Sunday shifts the focus from our sinful-
ness and need for conversion to the joy and hope that the advent of Jesus
should be for us. Isaiah tells us that even the desert will bloom and
"rejoice with joyful song." Don't be overwhelmed, the Lord says, with
your weakness. Rather, "Be strong, fear not! Here is your God, he
comes with vindication." God will bring healing to all the land and its
people.

James tells us that we must be as patient as the farmer waiting for
harvest and he recommends we take the prophets as models of patience.
The model that looms large again is John the Baptist. From his prison
cell he sends disciples to ask a central question of Jesus: "Are you the
one who is to come, or should we look for another?" Could it be that
John was experiencing fear and doubts and needed the hope and joy of
an affirmative answer from Jesus? Jesus answers by applying to himself
the prophecy of Isaiah about the signs of the messianic healing. And
then Jesus extols the person of John, and more—he gives me the good
news of what dignity is mine by the advent of God's kingdom: "The
least in the kingdom of heaven is greater than he." The joy and hope of
Advent is found in my renewing the gift of being a Christian in the new
dispensation. Let the desert within me "rejoice with joyful song."

SHARING

How do I help "those whose hearts are frightened" in our parish/community by saying in my whole consistency of life, "Be strong, fear not! Here is your God"?

Share any time in the last year when the patience of our small group/community (or another small group to which I belong) reaped harvest in the parish?

How have we as a small group/community taken a prophetic stand in the larger community?

Vatican II's document on the church and the world was entitled *Gaudium et spes*, meaning "Joy and Hope." How will we as a community, or as individuals, be a sign of joy and hope to others this week?

ACTION RESPONSE

Choose an action that will enable individuals or the group as a whole to live out in the coming week what has been shared.

PRAYER

Allow time for spontaneous prayer and conclude with praying the responsorial psalm of Sunday's liturgy, Psalm 146.

Fourth Sunday of Advent

OPENING PRAYER

The Alternative Opening Prayer of Today's Liturgy

READINGS: Isaiah 7:10–14; Romans 1:1–7; Matthew 1:18–24.

REFLECTION

Isaiah today tells us that the sign of the savior will be that a virgin shall bear a son and he shall be called Emmanuel—God with us. In the gospel it is repeated that Joseph is told to give that son a personal name, Jesus. He will save his people.

Emmanuel/Jesus—two power-filled, thought-provoking names. So many people complain about our computerized society. They are only faceless numbers with no name. Because God is with us in Jesus we do have a personal dignity and a name. As we prepare for the renewal of his coming may we be still and know God is with us in Jesus. And because of that name—Emmanuel/Jesus, we too are named in God. My personal name (Mary, John, etc.) is important and blessed in the Lord. Speak your name with gentleness and love just as the angel spoke to Joseph of the name of Jesus.

SHARING

How do we speak our names to each other with dignity and love in our small group/community?

Do I really believe that God's advent to me begins by calling me by name? Give an example of how you have experienced this.

How have I set aside quiet time at prayer this week to prepare for the coming of Emmanuel/Jesus?

ACTION RESPONSE

Choose an action that will enable individuals or the group as a whole to live out in the coming week what has been shared.

PRAYER

Allow time for spontaneous prayer and conclude with praying the responsorial psalm of Sunday's liturgy, Psalm 24.

CHRISTMAS SEASON

Sunday in the Octave of Christmas (Holy Family)

OPENING PRAYER

The Alternative Opening Prayer of Today's Liturgy

READINGS: Sirach 3:2–6; 12–14; Colossians 3:12–17;
Matthew 2:13–15; 19–23.

REFLECTION

As a small group/community we are called to be family to each other. Paul gives us some practical advice as a community. He counsels: "bearing with one another and forgiving one another…as the Lord has forgiven you." Then he tells us the secret: "Let the word of Christ dwell in you richly…teach and admonish one another."

A good deal of ministry in the parish is concerned with the word—education, formation, baptismal catechesis, marriage preparation, the Order of Christian Initiation of Adults. Our faith calls us to live the word in all aspects of our life—our family, small group/community, parish, work life.

SHARING

Do I allow patient time to listen to another's word? Give an example.

In regard to my commitments how am I a person of my word?

Share a word of encouragement that some member of your family spoke to you recently.

What will I do to share concretely with my family this week?

ACTION RESPONSE

Choose an action that will enable individuals or the group as a whole to live out in the coming week what has been shared.

PRAYER

Allow time for spontaneous prayer and conclude with praying the responsorial psalm of Sunday's liturgy, Psalm 128.

Second Sunday after Christmas

OPENING PRAYER

The Alternative Opening Prayer of Today's Liturgy

READINGS: Sirach 24:1–4, 8–12; Ephesians 1:3–6, 15–18;
John 1:1–18.

REFLECTION

This week Paul prays a beautiful prayer for his Ephesians: "I do
not cease giving thanks for you, remembering you in my prayers, that
the God of Our Lord Jesus Christ…may give you a spirit of wisdom and
revelation resulting in knowledge of him. May the eyes of [your] hearts
be enlightened." Perhaps in our community we take each other for
granted. Couldn't we thank God for each other and continue to thank
God for one another? We all help one another to develop and hone our
wisdom, insight and innermost vision, as truly as the Ephesians did
in Paul's time. Again, we are asked to live out these ideas of Pauline
community. Would we be willing to have a meeting of ours filmed to
show at Sunday mass? That's what Paul means. He cannot ask the
Ephesians to love one another if he hasn't already loved them first.

SHARING

Have we grown to be a small group/community this year? In what
ways?

Share a time when you have experienced the kind of community
Paul describes.

Spend a little time thanking each other for some gift or insight we have received during the past year.

Spend time this week remembering others in prayer.

ACTION RESPONSE

Choose an action that will enable individuals or the group as a whole to live out in the coming week what has been shared.

PRAYER

Allow time for spontaneous prayer and conclude with praying the responsorial psalm of Sunday's liturgy, Psalm 147.

Sunday After January 6
(Baptism of the Lord)

OPENING PRAYER

The Alternative Opening Prayer of Today's Liturgy

READINGS: Isaiah 42:1–4, 6–7; Acts 10:34–38;
Matthew 3:13–17.

REFLECTION

Isaiah was called the fifth evangelist by the early church scholars because he delineated so many facets of the personality of Jesus. Today's reading inserted on the feast of the Lord's baptism is no exception. Isaiah talks of the suffering servant who is called by God for the "victory of justice." Until that justice is established, the servant/messiah is "Not crying out, not shouting, not making his voice heard in the street." Then in two striking images Isaiah says of the servant, "A bruised reed he shall not break, and a smoldering wick he shall not quench."

Have you ever seen a broken branch holding on by the most fragile of threads? The servant, Jesus, will bind it up in a symbol of binding and healing of God's people. Like the poet Hopkins, he "will not loose this last strand of man."

Again, think of a sputtering candle. A strong wind or even breath will blow it out. But Jesus is pictured as cupping the tiny flame, and ever so gently breathing it back into flame. We are called by our baptism in Jesus to be God's instruments to bind, heal and breathe life into the wounded and discouraged peoples. The justice of the servant/Jesus begins with our being the servant church.

SHARING

Is there a group in a "dungeon, those who live in darkness" in our parish that we have neglected? Share with one another who that group may be.

Have I observed anyone recently "holding on by the most fragile threads"? Share the experience.

Share a personal experience of being the "bruised reed...and a smoldering wick"?

What are some specific ways that we as a small group/community can mirror a model of the servant church?

ACTION RESPONSE

Choose an action that will enable individuals or the group as a whole to live out in the coming week what has been shared.

PRAYER

Allow time for spontaneous prayer and conclude with praying the responsorial psalm of Sunday's liturgy, Psalm 29.

LENTEN SEASON

First Sunday of Lent

OPENING PRAYER

The Alternative Opening Prayer of Today's Liturgy

READINGS: Genesis 2:7–9; 3:1–7; Romans 5:12–19; Matthew 4:1–11.

REFLECTION

We begin one of the deepest liturgical rhythms of the church this week. The reality of sin and grace, death and resurrection, Adam and Jesus loom large before us for forty days. Something deep within us, mysterious yet real, responds to the call. See the great number of churchgoers who crowded our churches on last Wednesday for ashes. The ashes speak to something very primal in us that helps us to confront our mortality and limitations.

Maybe that's why Genesis and Matthew today connect on a similar temptation. In Eden the promise of the serpent was, "You will be like gods." To Jesus in the desert the devil promised instant security of bread, power beyond the human, and wealth untold.

The paradox is that in Jesus the temptation of the devil becomes a reality of God's love. In the new Adam we gain security, power and wealth beyond our wildest hope. Lent is a time to recall what we are through sin and yet hope what we can be through grace. An old spiritual classic said it all in its title: *Dust—Remember Thou Art Splendor*.

SHARING

What in my experience makes me believe in original sin?

On the other side of the coin, share an experience that has helped me believe that I have the grace of Christ.

What could we as a community do for Lent?

ACTION RESPONSE

Choose an action that will enable individuals or the group as a whole to live out in the coming week what has been shared.

PRAYER

Allow time for spontaneous prayer, and conclude with praying the responsorial psalm of Sunday's liturgy, Psalm 51.

Second Sunday of Lent

OPENING PRAYER

The Alternative Opening Prayer of Today's Liturgy

READINGS: Genesis 12:1–4a; 2 Timothy 1:8b–10;
Matthew 17:1–9.

REFLECTION

One of the great biblical themes is the journey. Genesis tells of the early story of Abraham (at age 75) and his wife, Sarah, being called to a journey toward a strange and unnamed land. The gospel journey to Jerusalem is interrupted by a transfiguration of Jesus on Tabor before Peter, James and John. For a moment the fullness of the Messiah transfigures the face and clothes of Jesus. Moses and Elijah were there and a voice is heard saying, "This is my beloved Son." But soon the vision was over and the three apostles "saw no one else but Jesus alone."

They then continued the journey, came down from Tabor and took the road to Jerusalem. In all the synoptic accounts, the transfiguration is sandwiched between two predictions of the passion and death of Jesus. The savior asked them to remember the glory of Tabor as a foretaste of the resurrection. But first there must be the journey to Calvary. The same three apostles will be with Jesus in the Garden of Gethsemane.

Our journey is easier because, unlike Peter, James and John, we already know the outcome of the Lord's journey. The transfiguration is the promise of Easter. But first, our journey, like that of the apostles, must encounter the mystery of the cross.

SHARING

What is this Lent saying new to me about my personal journey with Christ?

Where have I experienced transfigured moments in my life? Share some of those moments.

How have our sharings in this group/community helped to clarify my journey? Give a specific example.

How will I reach out this week to someone I know who is suffering in some way?

ACTION RESPONSE

Choose an action that will enable individuals or the group as a whole to live out in the coming week what has been shared.

PRAYER

Allow time for spontaneous prayer and conclude with praying the responsorial psalm of Sunday's liturgy, Psalm 33.

Third Sunday of Lent

OPENING PRAYER

The Alternative Opening Prayer of Today's Liturgy

READINGS: Exodus 17:3–7; Romans 5:1–2, 5–8; John 4:5–42.

REFLECTION

How human is the grumbling of the Israelites in their thirst for water during the exodus experience! They grumble about their journey. Why did they have to leave Egypt? At least there in their bondage they had water. God directs Moses to strike the rock at Horeb and water flows forth, but they had to move on and they would thirst again.

In the gospel of St. John, Jesus says the new Moses also asks the Samaritan woman for water, but he takes it to a new level—a new kind of water. Unlike the Israelites in the desert, this water is such that whoever drinks of it will never thirst again. Then Jesus explains, "The water I shall give will become in him a spring of water welling up to eternal life."

Jesus is using water as a symbol of the well of life within us which will slake the deepest spiritual thirst for meaning in our journey. The Samaritan woman tasted of this water of life in Jesus' acceptance of her. She left her old water jar behind and hurried to the town. There she spoke the good news and invited those whom she had avoided until now to come and see Jesus who told her who he was and gave her the new water of life. They came and tasted and "heard for themselves."

SHARING

Am I ever like the Israelites, grumbling about thirst for meaning and missing the invitation of Jesus to the well of life within? Share a time when this happened.

What is an experience in my life when I "tasted the living water" of life given to me by Jesus?

What can I do this week to carry the good news to others and invite them to come to know Jesus better?

ACTION RESPONSE

Choose an action that will enable individuals or the group as a whole to live out in the coming week what has been shared.

PRAYER

Allow time for spontaneous prayer and conclude with praying the responsorial psalm of Sunday's liturgy, Psalm 95.

Fourth Sunday of Lent

OPENING PRAYER

The Alternative Opening Prayer of Today's Liturgy

READINGS: 1 Samuel 16:1b, 6–7, 10–13a; Ephesians 5:8–14; John 9:1–41.

REFLECTION

All three readings today revolve around the theme of light and darkness, blindness and sight and, lastly, sight and insight. In Samuel when the Lord wants to choose a king from among the sons of Jesse he reminds us, "Not as a person sees does God see, because individuals see the appearances but the Lord looks into the heart." The Lord rejected all the sons until the youngest, David, was called in from shepherding. With divine insight the Lord says, "There—anoint him, for this is he!"

Paul tells the Ephesians that once they lived in darkness, but now, since they are in the light of the Lord, they should "live as children of light." Paul knows that unless we live in Christ's light we will drift back into the blindness of darkness and death.

In the gospel, John tells the long story of the man born blind whom Jesus heals. The Pharisees refuse to see it. They try to put the man down. They call him ignorant. They question his blindness. His only answer is, "One thing I do know is that I was blind and now I see." Later he meets Jesus and he responds to the Lord's invitation to believe in God. He moves from sight to the insight of faith while the Pharisees who have physical sight are blind to the faith in Jesus. Thus the paradox of Jesus: "I came into this world for judgment, so that those who do not see might see, and those who do see might become blind."

35

SHARING

How has our praying together helped us to share the same kind of insight the Lord manifests in the choice of David?

What does Paul mean when he calls us to be not only in the light but live as children of light?

How have we as a small group/community helped each other to move from sight to insight on any problem?

Spend some time this week reflecting on the "blind spots" in your life. Where is the Lord calling you to see in a new way?

ACTION RESPONSE

Choose an action that will enable individuals or the group as a whole to live out in the coming week what has been shared.

PRAYER

Allow time for spontaneous prayer and conclude with praying the responsorial psalm of Sunday's liturgy, Psalm 23.

Fifth Sunday of Lent

OPENING PRAYER

The Alternative Opening Prayer of Today's Liturgy

READINGS: Ezekiel 37:12–14; Romans 8:8–11; John 11:1–45.

REFLECTION

With only two weeks left before Easter, we could be flagging in our good resolves for the season of Lent. So to buoy up our spirits, the liturgy holds up the resurrection today as the goal of the cross. Paul is very consoling, reminding us that if the Spirit who raised Jesus from the dead really is alive in us then we, too, will share in the resurrection of Jesus. In the gospel Jesus uses the death of Lazarus as an opportunity to speak prophetically about the present resurrection. Jesus goes beyond the resurrection of the last day and says, "I am the resurrection and the life." Then to confirm his statement the Lord says "Lazarus, come out!"

Both Paul and Jesus talk about the present guarantee of the Spirit of Jesus living in us as the hope for the final resurrection. They are talking about now, for if the Spirit is alive in me, then I am already sharing in the risen life of Jesus. It is our self-appointed tombs of fear that keep us dead and bound up. The liturgy acclamation is "Christ has died, Christ is risen, Christ will come again." The central phrase in this acclamation emphasizes the *now* and is present tense.

SHARING

Do I believe and act as though Jesus has risen in my life? In our community? Share a recent example.

If I envisage myself as Lazarus bound in cloth but ready to be set free, what one thing would I do with my new-found freedom?

How do we apply to ourselves the words of Jesus to Martha, Mary and the crowd gathered around the risen Lazarus, "Untie him and let him go"?

How will we share risen moments with other people in our lives this week?

ACTION RESPONSE

Choose an action that will enable individuals or the group as a whole to live out in the coming week what has been shared.

PRAYER

Allow time for spontaneous prayer and conclude with praying the responsorial psalm of Sunday's liturgy, Psalm 130.

Passion Sunday (Palm Sunday)

OPENING PRAYER

The Alternative Opening Prayer of Today's Liturgy

READINGS: Isaiah 50:4–7; Philippians 2:6–11;
Matthew 26:14–66.

REFLECTION

Years ago Louis Evely said that when we read the gospel it should not be as an impersonal history of the past, but as a prophetic insight into my present journey. More recently, James Fowler in his *Stages of Faith*, shares that for years he tried to study and read the Bible with all the tools of modern biblical criticism. Only when he went into spiritual direction was he told to listen to the word with his heart. In his own phrase he tells us, "Rather than reading the word I let the word read me." We know there are a few people in our lives who can read us like a book. Today let the book of the gospel passion read us and tell us who we are. Isaiah says about the same in his first reading: "Morning after morning he opens my ear that I may hear."

So, today, let one of our group read the passion of Matthew to the others. The others will listen. But pray that the word today may read us.

SHARING

After the reading, take a time of silence and personal prayer, pondering the special word that spoke to your heart. When you're ready, share what you heard about yourself and perhaps the small group/ community.

If time permits, you may want to continue with the questions below.

QUESTIONS

Who are people in my life whom I consider as persons who can "read me like a book"?

What exactly is meant by, "Rather than reading the word, I let the word read me"?

During the week allow my behavior to reflect the "Word's having read me."

ACTION RESPONSE

Choose an action that will enable individuals or the group as a whole to live out in the coming week what has been shared.

PRAYER

Allow time for spontaneous prayer and conclude with praying the responsorial psalm of Sunday's liturgy, Psalm 22.

EASTER SEASON

Easter Sunday

OPENING PRAYER

The Alternative Opening Prayer of Today's Liturgy

READINGS: Acts 10:34a, 37–43; 1 Colossians 3:1–4;
John 20:1–9.

REFLECTION

In the gospel of Matthew, the angels at the tomb announce that Jesus is risen. Later in that same passage Jesus appears to the women himself as risen. Both Jesus and the angel conclude with the same command: "Then go quickly and tell his disciples…he is going before you to Galilee; there you will see him" (Mt 28:7).

Mark records the same command and John adds the twenty-first chapter to bring the disciples back to Galilee. Because he will continue the journey to Rome in Acts, Luke has the angel tell the disciples, "*Remember* what he said to you while he was still *in Galilee*" (Lk 24:6). And they remembered.

Why the instructions for a return to Galilee? It cannot be a matter of a literal geographical trip or of a physical seeing of Jesus. Rather, the disciples have to go back to Galilee in time and memory and recall all that Jesus said and did there. From the prism of the resurrection, the story and the journey fall together and make startling sense. This is how the gospels were first written.

The disciples had to turn to a deeper reflection on the events and teaching of Jesus in Galilee. T. S. Eliot says it beautifully, that we have to "know the place for the first time" and perhaps understand Jesus for the first time.

SHARING

What new insights have I gained this Lent concerning the death and resurrection of Jesus and its meaning in my life? Share your reflection with the group.

How am I living the teachings of Jesus in my relationships with others?

What will I do this week to carry the good news of Jesus to all I meet?

ACTION RESPONSE

Choose an action that will enable individuals or the group as a whole to live out in the coming week what has been shared.

PRAYER

Allow time for spontaneous prayer and conclude with Sunday's responsorial psalm, Psalm 118, or the Sequence (poetic text) of Easter, "To the Paschal Victim" (see Prayer Resources at the end of this book).

Second Sunday of Easter

OPENING PRAYER

The Alternative Opening Prayer of Today's Liturgy

READINGS: Acts 2:42–47; 1 Peter 1:3–9; John 20:19–31.

REFLECTION

In the original Greek of his gospel, John uses the word for faith 97 times, but always as a verb, never as a noun. A verb is the link between the subject "I" and the object "thou." The verb helps us to make new connections with different objects. A verb, unlike a noun, is not static; it moves; it grows. It's always in process.

So, in today's readings faith is highlighted. Thomas, who was not with the eleven has doubts, but when the risen Jesus appears, he makes the greatest statement of faith yet, "My Lord and my God!" Jesus speaks of us when he says, "Blessed are those who have not seen and have believed." We believe on the testimony of witnesses in apostolic times. John concludes, "But these are written that you may [come to] believe that Jesus is the Messiah…and that through this belief you may have life in his name."

In the experience of prayer, we can have affirmation of our faith and intimations of what we have heard from others, but ultimately our faith is that of Peter, "those who have not seen and have believed." God has gifted us with the precious gift of faith, but in a Johannine sense, faith must be a verb to grow and to make new connections in our life. "We have come to believe."

SHARING

In what way has some of my faith died to a new and mature faith? Share an example.

How has my faith been deepened by sharing in our community?

How does our community measure up against the first reading from the Acts of the Apostles?

What concrete action will I take this week to illuminate a new and mature faith?

ACTION RESPONSE

Choose an action that will enable individuals or the group as a whole to live out in the coming week what has been shared.

PRAYER

Allow time for spontaneous prayer and conclude with praying the responsorial psalm of Sunday's liturgy, Psalm 118.

Third Sunday of Easter

OPENING PRAYER

The Alternative Opening Prayer of Today's Liturgy

READINGS: Acts 2:14, 22–33; 1 Peter 1:17–21; Luke 24:13–35.

REFLECTION

In any of the detailed stories of the appearance of Jesus after his resurrection, those who encounter the savior do not in the beginning recognize him. In his risen form Jesus is so radically different that Mary thought him to be the gardener until the Lord says as only he can, "Mary." The apostles fishing at Galilee do not recognize the man until the new miraculous draught of fish. They know the risen Jesus in an act of connective memory—an event of the past is remembered and connected with the deed of the present.

Today, in the beautiful account of the disciples on the road to Emmaus, we encounter another example. The disciples experience Jesus who travels along with them only as a stranger. It is only when he explains the scripture and breaks bread that they recognize him in memory as the Lord.

Henri Nouwen is very fond of the word re-member as membering again, making a person or an event part of me at a deeper spiritual level. In some way all the Old and New Testaments are an extended act of re-membering the saving deeds of God and Jesus and making them alive in the now time.

One of the ways that I can experience Jesus in his risen form is to bring a word heard or read long ago into the present to be illuminated by the word. In that union of word and experience, I know Jesus in a new and risen way.

To help me in this quest we have the promise of the Holy Spirit, who is not only to teach but also "to recall all that I have told you." As real as such an experience can be, it is but a faint foretaste of what will be ours in the final resurrection.

SHARING

Have I ever experienced the Holy Spirit opening me up to the word so that my heart burned as the disciples did on the road to Emmaus? Share an experience of this.

How have we experienced "hearts burning" in this community?

How can we share our "burning hearts"?

How can we share with the larger parish community?

What are some creative possibilities?

ACTION RESPONSE

Choose an action that will enable individuals or the group as a whole to live out in the coming week what has been shared.

PRAYER

Allow time for spontaneous prayer and conclude with praying the responsorial psalm of Sunday's liturgy, Psalm 16.

Fourth Sunday of Easter

OPENING PRAYER

The Alternative Opening Prayer of Today's Liturgy

READINGS: Acts 2:14a, 36–41; 1 Peter 2:20b–25;
John 10:1–10.

REFLECTION

One of the tenderest images of God in the Old Testament is that of shepherd. None perhaps surpasses the beauty of the twenty-third psalm in today's responsorial. But, as always, Jesus goes beyond and personalizes it on a deeper level. Jesus tells us that he is the Good Shepherd who calls God's own by name. How often is this illustrated in the gospel! Jesus calls all of the apostles and disciples by name in the original invitation and when he dialogues with them. We think, too, of God's personal calls by name to Zaccheus, Lazarus, Saul, Mary.

We rarely call ourselves by our own name. Usually it is to scold ourselves. Why shouldn't I in prayer speak my name in gentleness and love? Why shouldn't I in reading scripture insert my name where the Lord will say "you"? So speak our names today gently and tenderly. Whisper it loud enough to hear it ourselves. Recall all the times and speak them when your name was spoken in baptism, confirmation, matrimony, religious commitment, graduations, loving greetings in person and on the phone, on birthday cards and letters. Speak your name at prayer time.

It will be a foretaste of what we hope to hear from the Good Shepherd at the end-time when God will call each of us by name and say to John and Mary, "Come blessed of my Father."

SHARING

Let someone read the Twenty-third Psalm aloud, and then let each one recount a part of it that resonates with his/her own experience.

Can I recall an experience when I appreciated someone calling me by name? Share the experience.

What specific action will I do this week to live out the call of the Good Shepherd?

ACTION RESPONSE

Choose an action that will enable individuals or the group as a whole to live out in the coming week what has been shared.

PRAYER

Allow time for spontaneous prayer and conclude with praying the responsorial psalm of Sunday's liturgy, Psalm 23.

Fifth Sunday of Easter

OPENING PRAYER

The Alternative Opening Prayer of Today's Liturgy

READINGS: Acts 6:1–7; 1 Peter 2:4–9; John 14:1–12.

REFLECTION

In the first reading from Acts we are given a model and challenge to the local church community of today. While the apostolic church was still very young, it felt the stress of growing pains. As new groups of gentiles came into the Jewish church, new problems arose.

The heart of the problem was bread. The Greek widows felt that they were being given less than the Jewish widows. Out of a small problem an important decision was made and an equally important principle disclosed. Rather than solving the problem at hand, the apostles decided that the distribution of bread was too much for them and was interfering with their main priority. So they asked the community to choose seven people to take over the ministry of the bread's distribution. They let go of it entirely so that their priority might be renewed—that is, to "Devote ourselves to prayer and to the ministry of the word."

Isn't that what our parish councils and committees should be doing? Willing parishioners who have talents could be called forth to minister to the many needs of our parishes. It means, of course, that those who may be doing too much are being asked to share those ministries and as leaders to concentrate on their chief function "prayer and to the ministry of the word." This is no small task and yet is the most important of priorities for leaders.

SHARING

As a community how do we discern those with talents and encourage them to respond to the call to ministry?

How would I explain prayer and ministry of the word today as the heart of parish or community leadership?

How are we helping our parish grow as a community of small communities?

Spend some time this week reflecting on someone in the parish community who needs to be called forth to use his/her gifts and talents. Take some time to talk with this person and encourage involvement.

ACTION RESPONSE

Choose an action that will enable individuals or the group as a whole to live out in the coming week what has been shared.

PRAYER

Allow time for spontaneous prayer and conclude with praying the responsorial psalm of Sunday's liturgy, Psalm 33.

Sixth Sunday of Easter

OPENING PRAYER

The Alternative Opening Prayer of Today's Liturgy

READINGS: Acts 8:5–8, 14–17; 1 Peter 3:15–18;
John 14:15–21.

REFLECTION

In John's gospel today, Jesus promises that the Holy Spirit will be with the church for all times. Not only will the Holy Spirit "be with you always," but he will also "be in you." The important words are "with you" and "always."

The apostolic church whose story is told in Luke's Acts certainly took full advantage of the Spirit in which they believed. Just read the certainty with which Peter and John imposed hands on the Samaritans in the first reading. Little wonder that Acts is sometimes referred to as the gospel of the Holy Spirit.

From time to time in history charismatic leaders, prophets, saints have lived fully in the reality of the power of the Spirit. Such was Pope John XXIII when he called for a new Pentecost in Vatican II.

The vision of Vatican II for the church was that the church should be a sign of joy and hope. We sometimes wonder where has all the joy and hope gone. But no one can box in the Holy Spirit in the local community. All the gifts are here and the same spirit Jesus promised is with us and within us.

If the local community is not a sign of the Spirit's presence in the dimension of joy and hope, we have no one to blame but ourselves.

SHARING

Am I aware of the Holy Spirit working within the people of our community? Give an example.

What experience have I had of the Holy Spirit in my own journey?

As a small group/community do we first seek the vision of the Holy Spirit in prayer before we solve problems on our own? Give an example of when this has happened.

How can we be a sign of joy and hope to others this week?

ACTION RESPONSE

Choose an action that will enable individuals or the group as a whole to live out in the coming week what has been shared.

PRAYER

Allow time for spontaneous prayer and conclude with praying the responsorial psalm of Sunday's liturgy, Psalm 66.

Seventh Sunday of Easter

OPENING PRAYER

The Alternative Opening Prayer of Today's Liturgy

READINGS: Acts 1:12–14; 1 Peter 4:13–16; John 17:1–11a.

REFLECTION

At the conclusion of his prayer in chapter 17 of John, Jesus says, "I pray for them." And then adds, "I pray not only for them, but also for those who will believe in me through their word" (Jn 17:20). It is no idle projection to say that Jesus included each of us in that prayer because over the centuries, the word given the apostles has finally come down to us and we believe through that same word.

This certainty was the conviction of the apostles themselves. From the first reading after the ascension of Jesus they returned to wait for the Holy Spirit. "They devoted themselves with one accord to prayer." They were responding and listening to the prayer of Christ. Nor was it just the apostles for, interestingly enough, "Some women, and Mary the mother of Jesus" were in their company.

Doesn't this tell us something about the power and priority of prayer in reference to Jesus who first prayed to the Father for us? Secondly, doesn't the Acts model tell us something important, too, about the community of men and women, apostles and disciples? It is from authentic prayer that authentic community arises, because at the last supper, Jesus prayed for all, who through the apostles, "Believed that you sent me."

SHARING

Do I fully realize that Jesus prayed for *me* at the last supper?

How does this realization make me feel?

How does my personal prayer affect the quality of our communal prayer?

How can we improve on the quality of prayer at our small group/community gatherings?

What specific action will I choose this week to deepen my personal prayer?

ACTION RESPONSE

Choose an action that will enable individuals or the group as a whole to live out in the coming week what has been shared.

PRAYER

Allow time for spontaneous prayer and conclude with praying the responsorial psalm of Sunday's liturgy, Psalm 27.

Pentecost Sunday

OPENING PRAYER

The Alternative Opening Prayer of Today's Liturgy

READINGS: Acts 2:1–11; 1 Corinthians 12:3b–7; 12–13;
                  John 20:19–23.

REFLECTION

Pentecost, the feast of the coming of the Holy Spirit, says different things to different people, and to each of us at different times of our lives.

Perhaps we can as a small group/community, look at two insights from the readings of the feast. First, Paul reminds us, "There are different...gifts but the same Spirit....To each individual the manifestation of the Spirit is given for one benefit....All the parts of the body, though many, are one body." It can act as a good checklist of the Spirit's operating in our community. One, do we recognize the variety of gifts in people? Two, do we use our gifts for the common good? Three, despite our differences, do we perceive that we form one body?

The second insight comes from Acts in describing the first Pentecostal experience of the apostles speaking to an assembly of people from all over the Mediterranean world. The people realized how different they were, yet those Galileans spoke and were understood by each group in their own language. "We hear them speaking in our own tongues of the mighty acts of God." This meant a miracle of language that can also be understood symbolically, that in every age the church must speak the eternal truths in a language people can understand.

In his opening address to the council, John XXIII saw this when he said, "The truths contained in the venerable body of doctrine is one thing. The way in which it is preached and presented is something else again." Do we as a small group/community try to speak the truth of the faith in the language of people today?

SHARING

How do I think our small group/community fares with the checklist of Paul about gifts, common good, and unity?

How do we as a parish community fare in the same checklist?

Share an example of how we can present the truths of our faith in a language that people can understand.

What will we do specifically this week to share the truths of our faith?

ACTION RESPONSE

Choose an action that will enable individuals or the group as a whole to live out in the coming week what has been shared.

PRAYER

Allow time for spontaneous prayer, and conclude with Sunday's beautiful Sequence (poetic text). (See Prayer Resources at the end of this book).

Trinity Sunday

OPENING PRAYER

The Alternative Opening Prayer of Today's Liturgy

READINGS: Exodus 34:4b–6, 8–9; 2 Corinthians 13:11–13;
                  John 3:16-18.

REFLECTION

A very popular form of escape literature is the detective mystery story. Somewhere in the last chapter the author lets us know the murderer was the butler. The mystery is solved and the story is over. All detective mysteries, however, are really problems to be solved.

The mystery of God is never a problem to be solved. Rather, God has chosen to reveal Godself out of goodness and wisdom (Eph 1:9) and to make known God's will for us. In that holy self-communication the scriptures reveal a triune God who is for us in mercy and love. We are called to friendship and commitment with the Holy Trinity.

So, the deepest core of who God is has been given to us in the revelation of the Holy Trinity. For many of us initiation into the divine mystery of the triune God comes first through the faith witness of our parents. For example, it was our parents who taught us how to make the sign of the cross. We were baptized in the threefold divine name. We begin and end our eucharist with the blessing of the Father, Son and Holy Spirit.

In today's epistle Paul concludes with a blessing that we use as a welcome in the beginning of the liturgy. "The grace of the Lord Jesus Christ and the love of God, and the fellowship of the Holy Spirit be with all of you."

SHARING

How would you try to explain the difference between a "whodunit" mystery and a mystery of our faith?

Are you able to identify a relationship with the Trinity in your life? How?

Do you think that Paul's description of the characteristics of the Trinity, namely: grace, love and friendship, speak to your experience?

ACTION RESPONSE

Choose an action that will enable individuals or the group as a whole to live out in the coming week what has been shared.

PRAYER

Allow time for spontaneous prayer and conclude with reading the responsorial psalm of Sunday's liturgy, Daniel 3:52–56.

Corpus Christi

OPENING PRAYER

The Alternative Opening Prayer of Today's Liturgy

READINGS: Deuteronomy 8:2–3, 14b–16a; 1 Corinthians
                  10:16–17; John 6:51–58.

REFLECTION

When he was struck on the road to Damascus, Paul was given an insight that he never forgot. While he lay on the ground, blinded by the light he heard a voice say, "Saul, Saul why do you persecute ME?" He learned early on that when he persecuted this or that follower of Jesus he was doing violence to the body of Christ. Paul began to see a close connection between the body of Jesus that he "broke" in the eucharist and the mystical body of Christ dwelling in one of his disciples.

He tells us, "The bread that we break, is it not a participation in the body of Christ?...we are one body, for we all partake of the one loaf." Fed by the eucharist Paul could more clearly see the body of Christ in himself and in others.

Like Paul we seek to grow in an integrated vision of the body of Christ in the sacrament and in people, whether saints or sinners. In the final judgment, Jesus speaks of his body in others. "I was hungry... naked...whatever you did for one of these least sisters or brothers of mine, you did for me" (Mt 25:35, 36, 40).

In order for us to be faithful in witness and service as Christ's disciples we need to be nourished regularly through the eucharistic presence of Christ. So our prayer is, "Lord help us to be faithful to your presence in eucharist and in all people."

SHARING

Do you ever experience the presence of Christ through others? Explain.

Share how the presence of Christ in the eucharist gives hope to your life each day.

What do you think Paul meant when he said, "We are one body, for we all partake of the one loaf?"

ACTION RESPONSE

Choose an action that will enable individuals or the group as a whole to live out in the coming week what has been shared.

PRAYER

Allow time for spontaneous prayer and conclude with reading the responsorial psalm of Sunday's liturgy, Psalm 147 or the Sequence.

SEASON OF THE YEAR (ORDINARY TIME)

Second Sunday of the Year

OPENING PRAYER

The Alternative Opening Prayer of Today's Liturgy

READINGS: Isaiah 49:3, 5–6; 1 Corinthians 1:1–3; John 1:29–34.

REFLECTION

In today's gospel, John patterns for us the journey of faith that is common to all of us. In the text, John the Baptist tells us very honestly, "I did not know him." John was baptizing with water and calling people to repentance and preparing for the Messiah. He was told by God that one day he would "see the Spirit come down and remain, he is the one who will baptize with the Holy Spirit." But then again comes the refrain, "I did not know him." Then the day of grace arrived, and the One he had called the Lamb of God was baptized by John and he saw the Spirit descend upon him.

At that moment John saw and understood. At last he did recognize Jesus as the Messiah. So John closes his testimony with the glorious statement, "Now I have seen and testified that he is the Son of God." I, too, must recognize in faith who Jesus really is for me. And this happens when I "see for myself." From that time on, my witness and teaching has new power—the power of faith in the Holy Spirit, which is the power to touch and move hearts.

SHARING

When did I begin to see for myself that Jesus is my Lord and savior? How do I relate to the first verse of the responsorial psalm?

Give an example of how we share our faith journey honestly and with humility so that it can touch the faith of the world community.

ACTION RESPONSE

Choose an action that will enable individuals or the group as a whole to live out in the coming week what has been shared.

PRAYER

Allow time for spontaneous prayer and conclude with praying the responsorial psalm of Sunday's liturgy, Psalm 40.

Third Sunday of the Year

OPENING PRAYER

The Alternative Opening Prayer of Today's Liturgy

READINGS: Isaiah 8:23–9:3; 1 Corinthians 1:10–13, 17;
Matthew 4:12–23.

REFLECTION

Matthew connects the first reading from Isaiah and the gospel. The light foretold by Isaiah appeared in Galilee, and Jesus, the Light of the World, spoke as a prophet. "Repent, for the kingdom of heaven is at hand." Almost immediately Jesus began to gather disciples in the first call to Peter, Andrew, James and John. They were fishermen, involved in their work when Jesus called them, "Come after me, and I will make you fishers of men." We are told that they abandoned boat, nets and family ties and followed the Lord.

Much would happen in the years ahead. These four would follow, but at a most erratic pace. And finally, with the exception of John, they deserted Jesus at the end of his life. Only after the resurrection would they return to the journey of abandonment begun years before in Galilee.

But they never forgot the first call. All that would happen after Pentecost was to be built on the early vocation. In troubled times, as today's are, people are told to "camp afresh at the wellspring of your first call." Perhaps we could spend some quiet time in doing just that.

SHARING

How have I encouraged other people to get in touch with that holy moment of their beginning call to follow Jesus?

Share the first gentle call of the Lord in your life journey.

In your daily relationships of this week with whom will you share the call of the Lord in your life journey?

ACTION RESPONSE

Choose an action that will enable individuals or the group as a whole to live out in the coming week what has been shared.

PRAYER

Allow time for spontaneous prayer and conclude with praying the responsorial psalm of Sunday's liturgy, Psalm 27.

Fourth Sunday of the Year

OPENING PRAYER

The Alternative Opening Prayer of Today's Liturgy

READINGS: Zephaniah 2:3; 3:12–13; 1 Corinthians 1:26–31;
Matthew 5:1–12a.

REFLECTION

From a purely worldly viewpoint, the beatitudes border on the ridiculous. Gradually, for the Christian who tries to become a disciple, they move into the realm of paradox. And we become finally truly blessed when they become the new reality of our journey. It is interesting to note that with the exception of the first and eighth beatitude in Matthew, the others all refer to the future kingdom. But the first and eighth refer to the *now* kingdom, "theirs is the kingdom of heaven."

The first beatitude which guarantees the reign of God now is the most basic, "Blessed are the poor in spirit, theirs is the kingdom of heaven." From experience we know many people who are spiritually poor but who are far from blessed. They wallow in their depression and, like Sartre, see no exit, no meaning, no hope. Yet, we see others, too, who live the true meaning of poverty of spirit. They accept their limitations, and surrender totally to God. The outcome they experience is peace, freedom, even joy—all hallmarks of the reign of God.

If you've ever attended an AA (Alcoholics Anonymous) meeting, you hear people admit being powerless over alcohol and then turning their life and will over to the care of God to experience what they term a spiritual awakening. Once we have known the first beatitude at heart level, and experienced it, we can dare to live out the paradox of the other seven.

SHARING

Share a time when you lived poverty of spirit, that is, you truly depended upon God.

What other beatitudes do I particularly relate to from my own experience?

Is there a way in which members of a community can experience a group poverty of spirit? Give an example.

How can we help others experience peace, freedom, joy this week?

ACTION RESPONSE

Choose an action that will enable individuals or the group as a whole to live out in the coming week what has been shared.

PRAYER

Allow time for spontaneous prayer and conclude with praying the responsorial psalm of Sunday's liturgy, Psalm 146.

Fifth Sunday of the Year

OPENING PRAYER

The Alternative Opening Prayer of Today's Liturgy

READINGS: Isaiah 58:7–10; 1 Corinthians 2:1–5; Matthew 5:13–16.

REFLECTION

The theme of the readings today is light seen in action. Jesus tells us to let our light of good deeds shine before others so that "they may see your good deeds and glorify your heavenly Father." We become carriers of the light to lead others, not to ourselves, but to the common source.

Isaiah's words are particularly incisive. Note he uses prior action three times as a condition that "light shall break forth," that "your wound shall quickly be healed...The Lord will answer" your call. "Gloom shall become for you like midday." In each instance there is a prior condition to what follows in three "thens." How much the conditions sound like Jesus, "Sharing bread with the hungry, sheltering the oppressed and the homeless; clothing the naked...and not turning your back on your own...remove from your midst oppression, false accusation and malicious speech."

What a beautiful linkage between the Hebrew and Christian scriptures. An action done out of love and mature responsibility produces the same light for Isaiah and Jesus, and we dare to add, ourselves. For the Lord says to each of us, "*You* are the light of the world."

SHARING

Share an experience when I have seen this kind of light in the actions of another person.

When have I experienced that light through one of my own actions with the Lord?

How can we as a community be a source of light for others?

ACTION RESPONSE

Choose an action that will enable individuals or the group as a whole to live out in the coming week what has been shared.

PRAYER

Allow time for spontaneous prayer and conclude with praying the responsorial psalm of Sunday's liturgy, Psalm 112.

Sixth Sunday of the Year

OPENING PRAYER

The Alternative Opening Prayer of Today's Liturgy

READINGS: Sirach 15:15–20; 1 Corinthians 2:6–10;
Matthew 5:17–37.

REFLECTION

It almost seems to be the sad story of all societies and religions that in time they tend to give way to an exclusive external obedience to the law. Meanwhile, their hearts withhold interior obedience and love. So Jesus asks his followers to surpass the holiness of the scribes and Pharisees of his day, where they are satisfied with abstaining from murder, adultery, and unnecessary oaths. Jesus asks for a heart that will abstain as well from anger, lustful desires and any oath at all.

Paul tells us in Corinthians that "God has revealed" the deeper wisdom, "To us through the Spirit." So later on in that epistle in the thirteenth chapter, he gets to the heart of the matter, the motive behind doing a good deed, and abstaining from an evil one. Always the question is the motive. Why am I doing, or not doing, such and such? Paul tells us even "If I give away everything I own…but do not have love, I gain nothing" (1 Cor 13:3). But Jesus counters by telling us when we give a cup of water in his name, we merit the kingdom.

Only God can know the motive of our heart. And God can and does reveal that motive with the wisdom of self-knowledge through the Holy Spirit. So we cry, Holy Spirit teach us to be pure of heart.

SHARING

When have I chosen to follow my own conscience over the expectations of others?

How do I live according to my conscience every day?

Has our sharing in the small group/community challenged my motives at times during the past year? Give an example.

Spend some time this week reflecting on motives—why am I doing what I do?

ACTION RESPONSE

Choose an action that will enable individuals or the group as a whole to live out in the coming week what has been shared.

PRAYER

Allow time for spontaneous prayer and conclude with praying the responsorial psalm of Sunday's liturgy, Psalm 119.

Seventh Sunday of the Year

OPENING PRAYER

The Alternative Opening Prayer of Today's Liturgy

READINGS: Leviticus 19:1–2, 17–18; 1 Corinthians 3:16–23; Matthew 5:38–48.

REFLECTION

If we truly believe in what Paul tells us—that we are temples of God and the Spirit of God dwells within us—we would always love ourselves and others. But the practical fact is we always find an excuse to hold back love toward another person, ourselves or some group. Jesus commands us to love our enemies, to pray for our persecutors. He is not impressed that we love those who are good to us, as he says, "Do not the tax collectors do the same?" No, he insists it is only when I can't love of my own power that I realize that all love is a gift. A character in Graham Greene's *Burned Out Case* says, "We use the expression, don't we, 'Make love.' We can't make love. All we can do is share or respond to it. It is a gift."

When I can honestly say I can't love this one or that one, I am making some progress. Once more, I admit my poverty. So, we have to let God love the other through me. I will bear the gift of love and direct that gift of love to this enemy of mine. I begin to understand the wisdom of St. Francis when he prayed, "Lord, make me an instrument of your peace...let me sow love." The mystery is that the gift of love will touch others, and in the process, I myself may be healed by the gift I bear.

SHARING

I am praying to be an instrument of love. How am I doing? Share your response.

Am I amazed how parents can continue to love their teenagers during their difficult years? How do I account for it?

Do I ever feel like the enemy, or see one of my family or people I meet as an enemy? What do I do?

Who do I want the Lord to love through me this week?

ACTION RESPONSE

Choose an action that will enable individuals or the group as a whole to live out in the coming week what has been shared.

PRAYER

After spontaneous prayer, pray together the *Prayer of St. Francis of Assisi* (see Prayer Resources at the end of this book).

Eighth Sunday of the Year

OPENING PRAYER

The Alternative Opening Prayer of Today's Liturgy

READINGS: Isaiah 49:14–15; 1 Corinthians 4:1–5;
Matthew 6:24–34.

REFLECTION

Isaiah and Matthew combine with two of the most beautiful expressions of God's tender caring providence. Isaiah is most direct, "Can a mother forget her infant? I will never forget you." We all forget in difficult times that God always remembers us.

Jesus approaches God's providential care with a striking illustration of how the creator cares for the wildflowers and the birds of the air. Then, like Isaiah, he concludes "will he not much more provide for you?" Jesus tells us we have confused our priorities. We put food and clothes first and give inordinate time to worry. The real priority is "seek first the kingdom [of God]...and all these things will be given you besides." It takes faith and courage to put God's reign first with trust in God's providence to work with us to provide the other things as well. We see it in the lives of the saints, and in the risk prophetic people take in our times, and most frequently in the priorities of our parents and their parents before them. God is talking directly to me when saying, "O you of little faith...do not worry."

SHARING

Who is someone in my own family who risked the right priority and was happy?

Share a risk you took in keeping a priority and how the Lord provided.

How have I sometimes worried too much and neglected seeking God's reign first?

How will we specifically "re-member the forgotten" in our parish this week?

ACTION RESPONSE

Choose an action that will enable individuals or the group as a whole to live out in the coming week what has been shared.

PRAYER

Allow time for spontaneous prayer and conclude with praying the responsorial psalm of Sunday's liturgy, Psalm 62.

Ninth Sunday of the Year

OPENING PRAYER

The Alternative Opening Prayer of Today's Liturgy

READINGS: Deuteronomy 11:18, 26–28; Romans 3:21–25, 28; Matthew 7:21–27.

REFLECTION

There's a great temptation to fall into the either/or trap when so often in life and religion we are challenged to be a both/and person. Occasionally, some fundamentalist preacher will still scream on television, "Faith alone and that's that." Both Moses and Jesus today ask for both hearing and acting on faith. Moses tells his people to "take these words of mine into your heart and soul" (Dt 11:18). "I set before you, this day, a blessing and curse: a blessing for obeying…a curse if you do not obey" (Dt 26–28). That's good direct Jewish logic.

Jesus tells us it takes more than saying, "Lord, Lord" (Mt 7:21) to enter God's reign. One must also do "the will of my Father" (Mt 7:21). So Jesus says we must both hear the word *and* put it into practice. The example he uses is on what foundation do I build my house—rock or sand? When rainstorms come the house built on rock survives; that on sand collapses. The one who hears the word *and* puts it into practice, has a foundation of rock. The one who just thinks he hears and does nothing is the sand person. It might help to reverse the old axiom, "practice what you preach" to read, "preach only what I practice."

SHARING

Who are some of the both/and people I admire in the modern church?

What is missing in me when I am just a "do-gooder"?

What are some ways in my spiritual journey where I have begun to listen and practice the word?

What action will I do this week to put my faith into action?

ACTION RESPONSE

Choose an action that will enable individuals or the group as a whole to live out in the coming week what has been shared.

PRAYER

Allow time for spontaneous prayer and conclude with praying the responsorial psalm of Sunday's liturgy, Psalm 31.

Tenth Sunday of the Year

OPENING PRAYER

The Alternative Opening Prayer of Today's Liturgy

READINGS: Hosea 6:3–6; Romans 4:18–25; Matthew 9:9–13.

REFLECTION

Every now and then we have to hear the prophetic word of the Lord saying things like, "Alfie, what's it all about? Are you missing the heart of the matter? Are you still straining out the gnat and letting the camel pass through?" In the first reading, Hosea sets us straight, "What can I do with you, Ephraim?" "Your piety is like…dew that early passes away." "It is love I desire, not sacrifice, and knowledge of God rather than holocausts." What he is saying is, first things first.

In the gospel, Jesus echoes the words of Hosea. The Pharisees missed the point of God's mercy in criticizing Jesus for eating with tax collectors who don't abide by the fullness of the law. Jesus overhears their remarks and hits them as teacher where they are most vulnerable, "Go and learn the meaning of the words; 'I desire mercy, not sacrifice.'" Jesus sends them back to their books with a final salvo, "I did not come to call the righteous but sinners." Can you imagine the joy of Matthew and all his union of tax collectors at supper when they heard this loving defense and acceptance of them? I like to think Matthew smiled and said, "More wine, Jesus?"

SHARING

How has Vatican II helped me grow to see what's central in our Catholic tradition?

As community members have we been conscious of keeping the balance of first things first? Share an example.

What will we as a community do this week to live the call of Jesus in the world to be people of mercy?

ACTION RESPONSE

Choose an action that will enable individuals or the group as a whole to live out in the coming week what has been shared.

PRAYER

Allow time for spontaneous prayer and conclude with praying the responsorial psalm of Sunday's liturgy, Psalm 50.

Eleventh Sunday of the Year

OPENING PRAYER

The Alternative Opening Prayer of Today's Liturgy

READINGS: Exodus 19:2–6a; Romans 5:6–11;
Matthew 9:36—10:8.

REFLECTION

Sometimes, as today, the readings present such rich images and truths that it is best we read them very slowly and pause to drink in the richness of God's gift.

In Exodus, God speaks to Moses, "Say to the house of Jacob; tell the Israelites: You have seen for yourselves how…I bore you up on eagle wings and brought you here to myself…If you harken to my voice…you shall be to me a kingdom of priests." (Repeat this paragraph and then pause.)

In Romans, Paul tells us it's precisely in this that God proves his love for us that "while we were still sinners, Christ died for us." (Repeat the paragraph and pause.)

In Matthew we are told, "At the sight of the crowds, his heart was moved with pity." They were lying prostrate from exhaustion, "Like sheep without a shepherd." "The kingdom of God is at hand." "Without cost you have received; without cost you are to give." (Repeat the paragraph and pause.)

SHARING

Three people in the group will volunteer to take each reading from Exodus, Romans and Matthew in order.

Read aloud and then share some insight received.

As a small group/community, share any way in which our larger community could be opened up to such an experience of the breaking of the bread of the word as we have experienced it this day?

What will we do this week to help others experience the richness of breaking open the word of God?

ACTION RESPONSE

Choose an action that will enable individuals or the group as a whole to live out in the coming week what has been shared.

PRAYER

Allow time for spontaneous prayer and conclude with praying the responsorial psalm of Sunday's liturgy, Psalm 100.

Twelfth Sunday of the Year

OPENING PRAYER

The Alternative Opening Prayer of Today's Liturgy

READINGS: Jeremiah 20:10–13; Romans 5:12–15;
Matthew 10:26–33.

REFLECTION

When the RENEW Process was first started years ago in the Newark Archdiocese, many people said the song that they most remembered from the program was *Be Not Afraid*. That is as it should be because fear is the most universal block to God's life in us. The word "fear" ranks number one in frequency of appearance in both the Old and New Testaments. The only way to dislodge fear is to trust in the Lord.

Jeremiah hears all those around him waiting for his downfall, but he doesn't fear because "the Lord is with me, like a mighty champion: my persecutors will stumble." "For to you, I have entrusted my cause." John tells us that in love there can be no fear. The theme that runs throughout the Bible is to let trust in God's love expel all of our fears.

Jesus is most direct in his advice to the apostles, "Do not be afraid of them." "And do not be afraid of those who kill the body but cannot kill the soul." "So do not be afraid." His basis is very simply that our lives are the concern of our loving God. We are in God's hands. We are not alone. Like Paul, we have to sing out fearlessly that nothing can "separate us from the love of God in Christ Jesus" (Rom 8:39). And that includes the number one killer, fear.

SHARING

When have I in fear surrendered in trust to God and discovered peace?

Share another scripture reading that I have found a source of strength in time of fear?

How have I been helped to dissipate some of my fears by this small group/community?

In what situations this week will I be a person of trust instead of fear?

ACTION RESPONSE

Choose an action that will enable individuals or the group as a whole to live out in the coming week what has been shared.

PRAYER

Allow time for spontaneous prayer and conclude with praying the responsorial psalm of Sunday's liturgy, Psalm 69.

Thirteenth Sunday of the Year

OPENING PRAYER

The Alternative Opening Prayer of Today's Liturgy

READINGS: 2 Kings 4:8–11, 14–16a; Romans 6:3–4, 8–11;
Matthew 10:37–42.

REFLECTION

Over the years, the word and reality of hospitality has been
watered down to mean doing something out of manners as is expected,
like serving someone tea and cookies. But it has a much deeper
significance. Because Christians saw Jesus in the sick, Christian
hospitality eventually led to the formation of hospitals. The medieval
monasteries that offered lodging to pilgrims had a motto over their main
door, "Hospes Venit, Christus Venit" ("When the guest comes, it is
Christ who comes.") So hospitality is not just rendering the expected
minimum service stemming from good manners, but it is being host or
hostess to the guest, Christ, stemming from the gospel.

Today both readings touch on authentic hospitality. Elisha is a
guest given the freedom of the house because he is a holy man. His
presence begets new life in the hostess, a Shunammite woman, when
she is blessed by God with the promise of a baby.

Jesus zeros in on the heart of hospitality, "Whoever receives you,
receives me." Like the home where Elisha stayed the guest who is
received as Christ will always bring the blessing of Christ to the host.

So says Jesus, "And whoever gives only a cup of cold water...will
surely not lose his reward." So in the climate of authentic hospitality,
both the host and the guest receive new life. There are no losers.

SHARING

Share some time when we experienced an authentic gospel hospitality.

As members of a small group/community how do we provide for planning practical helps to hospitality in the larger group/community?

In my family, neighborhood, workplace, how do I practice hospitality for others?

What specific action will you choose to do this week in response to the call to create hospitality?

ACTION RESPONSE

Choose an action that will enable individuals or the group as a whole to live out in the coming week what has been shared.

PRAYER

Allow time for spontaneous prayer and conclude with praying the responsorial psalm of Sunday's liturgy, Psalm 89.

Fourteenth Sunday of the Year

OPENING PRAYER

The Alternative Opening Prayer of Today's Liturgy

READINGS: Zechariah 9:9–10; Romans 8:9, 11–13; Matthew 11:25–30.

REFLECTION

In this beautiful prayer in today's gospel Jesus thanks and praises God for, "Although you have hidden these things from the wise and the learned you have revealed them to the children." We have a tendency to hear only the, "Shrewd as serpents" and forget the, "Simple as doves" which Jesus calls to live in tandem and tension (Mt 10:16). But for today, let's look at the dove side, the child in us.

The child with ordinary love and trust from his parents is very aware of life. The child is a person of wonder and stands in awe before the ordinary. Psychologists tell us that in each of us is a child, sometimes stunted and deprived, most often afraid to come out and to play as an adult. If we're lucky, we live long enough to rediscover our child and to recapture the awe and wonder of our early life. One of the advantages of growing old, like myself, is that when I give the sign of peace to little children in the crying room on Sunday, I see how a smile or an open hand moves them to a trusting response, and this is a very rich gift to me that evokes trust in the child within me.

Jesus tells us that being childlike (not childish) is a condition to entering the reign of God. Unless my child hears, there can be no response and trust when Jesus says, "Come to me, all you who labor and are burdened, and I will give you rest." Have you given your inner child a hug today?

SHARING

What are some specific joyful memories I had as a child? How am I in contact with my inner child?

As a group, do we ever play or recreate together? In what ways?

If, as a group, we have not recreated together, do we think it is a good idea? What would be the benefit or outcome of recreating together?

How will I initiate "play" with others this week?

ACTION RESPONSE

Choose an action that will enable individuals or the group as a whole to live out in the coming week what has been shared.

PRAYER

Allow time for spontaneous prayer and conclude with praying the responsorial psalm of Sunday's liturgy, Psalm 145.

Fifteenth Sunday of the Year

OPENING PRAYER

The Alternative Opening Prayer of Today's Liturgy

READINGS: Isaiah 55:10–11; Romans 8:18–23;
Matthew 13:1–23 or 13:1–9.

REFLECTION

If we are open and listen to the experience of the way other people break the word of God in their lives, it can oftentimes help us to hear the word in our own journey. Two insights which I experienced from others about today's readings I'd like to share. One time in a small dialogue homily a sister shared that she used to think, reflecting on Matthew's text, that she had moved from the first category, that is the seed on the path, to the fourth of the good soil, but as she grew more mature and honest she realized she was still partly in all four categories. She still didn't want to hear some parts of the gospel. Others she didn't stay with. There were parts which were still choked by dissipation of efforts, and a precious few ideas or seeds lodged in the good soil of her heart. I have to say, Amen, to her insight and how it affirms my own experience.

The other insight stems from the Isaiah text which says, the word "shall not return to me void." We never know the moment when there will be a breakthrough of our baptismal "Ephphata!" (Mk 7:34). A woman lector in one of my parishes really used to take the readings seriously. She would study and pray on the word of Sunday all week, and when she read, her word and the gospel were one and had power as it was proclaimed. After one of the Sunday liturgies, she came to me brimming with joyful tears. Following mass a man from the congregation, equally teared up, told her, "When you read today, it was the first time I ever heard the word of God." "Ephphata!"

SHARING

How do I relate to either of these insights from my own experience?

Can I come up with an appropriate experience on the word from my own journey? Share your response.

How willing are we to serve as lectors or participate in other liturgical ministry?

What specific ways will we proclaim the word this week?

ACTION RESPONSE

Choose an action that will enable individuals or the group as a whole to live out in the coming week what has been shared.

PRAYER

Allow time for spontaneous prayer and conclude with praying the responsorial psalm of Sunday's liturgy, Psalm 65.

Sixteenth Sunday of the Year

OPENING PRAYER

The Alternative Opening Prayer of Today's Liturgy

READINGS: Wisdom 12:13, 16–19; Romans 8:26–27
                  Matthew 13:24-43 or 13:24–30.

REFLECTION

I was at a Bible convention some years ago and noticed a number of people who were wearing buttons which read "PBPWMGINDWMY." At last, curiosity got the better of me and I asked one person what the button stood for. They smiled and said, "It stands for 'Please be patient with me. God is not done with me yet.'" Another way of saying that God never stops working, never gives up on us as imperfect creatures.

If many historical reformers of the past and some fundamentalists of the present had their way, the church would be only for the elite, the perfect, the saint. The church, thank God, is a pilgrim church, seeking to know the perfection of Christ, but always stumbling in its journey. Newman said, "How can we expect a perfect church with imperfect people?" This is not to say we condone or are indifferent to sin, but it is to say loudly that the church of Christ must always find room for the weak and the sinner as well as for the strong and the saintly.

This is the heart of Jesus' parable today. It would be so easy to pull up all the weeds, but the master in the story said, "No, if you pull up the weeds you might uproot the wheat along with them." He was willing as is Christ to wait patiently until harvest when the final separation will be made. The theology of the church goes even beyond it. For the miracle of the reign of God is that the weeds can be transformed into wheat even at the eleventh hour.

SHARING

How has patience paid off for a radical change in my life?
What kind of patience do I need in my life now?
What can we do to keep in mind the needs of all people?

ACTION RESPONSE

Choose an action that will enable individuals or the group as a whole to live out in the coming week what has been shared.

PRAYER

Allow time for spontaneous prayer and conclude with praying the responsorial psalm of Sunday's liturgy, Psalm 86.

Seventeenth Sunday of the Year

OPENING PRAYER

The Alternative Opening Prayer of Today's Liturgy

READINGS:

1 Kings 3:5, 7–12; Romans 8:28–30;
Matthew 13:44–52.

REFLECTION

One of the problems we may all face in life is the moment when someone cries out, "Why has God done this to me?" It may involve a sudden and tragic accident to a father of four, a lingering cancer death to a young mother, or the drowning of a child.

It is a time, not for theologizing, but one of patient presence. It is a time for the request of Solomon in the first reading for "an understanding heart." Later, there has to be follow-up at the right time, again demanding the understanding heart. Eventually, after the funeral is over and the deepest questions are asked, it may be the right time for gentle teaching about who God is, and more importantly who God is not. In time we learn that God does not send tragedy and sickness, but in the presence of it, God may be our only strength. It is this stage that Paul refers to when he says, "We know that all things work for good for those who love God."

From our own experience we know one of the best ways to illustrate the abstract is to share part of our story. The understanding heart becomes the wounded healer.

It takes a lot of wisdom, patience and time, but the ministry of the understanding heart is one that is most needed in our parish communities.

SHARING

How have I worked through in my own life the stages of dying (denial, anger, bargaining, depression and acceptance) described in Kübler-Ross' *Death and Dying* ?

How do I respond to people who cry out "why" in time of crisis?

As a community how could we reach out to those experiencing grief?

As an action response, share ideas about developing a grief-sharing group where people at different stages can be helped by the experiences of each other.

ACTION RESPONSE

Choose an action that will enable individuals or the group as a whole to live out in the coming week what has been shared.

PRAYER

Allow time for spontaneous prayer and conclude with praying the responsorial psalm of Sunday's liturgy, Psalm 119.

Eighteenth Sunday of the Year

OPENING PRAYER

The Alternative Opening Prayer of Today's Liturgy

READINGS: Isaiah 55:1–3; Romans 8:35, 37–39;
                  Matthew 14:13–21.

REFLECTION

We have all experienced those days when we were burned out and were so happy to settle back to watch our favorite television program and then that necessary relaxation was interrupted. The phone rang, or the doorbell, and we had to respond. Our plans for taking it easy went with that invader.

I think that's why we can relate so much to the gospel today. Jesus had just heard of the death of John the Baptist. He grieved for him, and "withdrew in a boat to a deserted place by himself." The people with a built-in radar system spotted Jesus crossing the lake, and they went around the end of the lake and were waiting for him in large numbers when he disembarked. He must have seen them at a distance and might have been tempted just to drift away to the center. But "When he disembarked and saw the vast crowd, his heart was moved with pity for them." He taught and healed well into the evening, and when the disciples told him to let them go to get something in the village, Jesus said, "Give them some food yourselves." They brought what they could scare up. Jesus blessed it and the disciples distributed it. It is interesting to see how Jesus changes his plans, manifests again his true priorities, and uses the bread as an occasion to call the disciples to shared responsibility.

97

SHARING

How do I feel when I have been interrupted by someone with a need?

How do I apply, "Give them some food yourselves" in my own life?

How can we as a community fit into the scenario of the gospel?

How will we "give something to eat" to others this week?

ACTION RESPONSE

Choose an action that will enable individuals or the group as a whole to live out in the coming week what has been shared.

PRAYER

Allow time for spontaneous prayer and conclude with praying the responsorial psalm of Sunday's liturgy, Psalm 145.

Nineteenth Sunday of the Year

OPENING PRAYER

The Alternative Opening Prayer of Today's Liturgy

READINGS: 1 Kings 19:9a, 11–13a; Romans 9:1–5;
Matthew 14:22–33.

REFLECTION

Hebrew is a primitive language and frequently has only one word for many situations. *Ruah*, for instance, can mean wind, breath or spirit. In the creation story the divine Ruah moved over the water as wind, God breathed the divine Ruah into the clay, and humankind became an image of the divine Ruah, Spirit. In the new creation of Pentecost, the Holy Spirit came as mighty wind, and gentle breath when Jesus appeared to the apostles after the resurrection.

So in the two readings today the Ruah idea is used differently. In the gospel a mighty wind caused panic on the lake as the apostles' boat was tossed about. When Jesus finally joins them in the boat, "the wind died down," but Jesus chides them for the lack of faith during the windy storm at sea.

In the first reading, it is just the opposite. Elijah waits for the word or appearance of the Lord. There was wind, earthquake and fire, but each time the text reads "that the Lord was not in the wind...earthquake ...fire." Then the divine Ruah comes as breath. "There was a tiny whispering sound. When he heard this, Elijah hid his face in his cloak and went and stood at the entrance of the cave." He knew God was present in the whisper.

Sometimes we are blind or tone deaf to catch Jesus in the

maelstrom of a storm or in the quiet whisper of a small prayer or call. God is present both in wind and whisper.

SHARING

In which of the two, wind or whisper, do I more frequently experience the Lord?

Give an example where I missed the Lord at the time and only realized God's presence in later reflection?

In my busy life am I sensitive to the Lord moving in both ways as wind and whisper? Give an example.

Reflect this week on the presence of the Lord in the wind and whisper situations of your life right now. Determine how you will respond.

ACTION RESPONSE

Choose an action that will enable individuals or the group as a whole to live out in the coming week what has been shared.

PRAYER

Allow time for spontaneous prayer and conclude with praying the responsorial psalm of Sunday's liturgy, Psalm 85.

Twentieth Sunday of the Year

OPENING PRAYER

The Alternative Opening Prayer of Today's Liturgy

READINGS: Isaiah 56:1, 6–7; Romans 11:13–15, 29–32;
Matthew 15:21–28.

REFLECTION

Once again Jesus tries to get away. This time it is from the
Pharisees and scribes who hound him about not keeping the traditions
of his religion. So the text begins, "Jesus...withdrew." He went beyond
the pale of the Jew to Tyre and Sidon, and don't you know even there he
will run into a problem. This time it is a Canaanite woman, a non-Jew,
who asks him to cure her daughter.

Almost as if Jesus were tired out from arguing with the Pharisees,
he seems to feel that maybe if I ignore her, she'll go away. The text
reads, "But he did not say a word in answer to her." When the disciples
returned, they said, "Send her away, for she keeps calling out after us."
But Jesus reasserts his mission is for Israel, and then the story continues.
In the rugged banter of the Middle East, Jesus adapts a Jewish saying to
the woman who asks for help that, "It is not right to take the food of the
children and throw it to the dogs." But in the game of give-and-take, she
is not so easily cornered. She counters with a quick, witty turn of phrase,
"Please, Lord, for even the dogs eat the scraps that fall from the table of
their masters."

Jesus accepts her trump card. "O woman, great is your faith! Let it
be done for you as you wish." And, of course, the daughter was healed.

It is an interesting story that reveals so much about the humanity and compassion of Jesus. It will be a preview of the Lord's last command to the apostles, "Make disciples of all nations" (Mt 28:19). It all begins when Jesus tried to get away from his fellow Israelites and in the deepest sense met us as Gentiles in the Canaanite woman.

SHARING

How do I fare with people who will not take no for an answer?

Do I have any people in my life I really consider not "our kind"?

Share your response. How am I being called to change my attitude toward them?

How are we as a community doing in work beyond the confines of our small group/community in the parish or community?

How can we as a group specifically address issues of injustice?

ACTION RESPONSE

Choose an action that will enable individuals or the group as a whole to live out in the coming week what has been shared.

PRAYER

Allow time for spontaneous prayer and conclude with praying the responsorial psalm of Sunday's liturgy, Psalm 67.

Twenty-First Sunday of the Year

OPENING PRAYER

The Alternative Opening Prayer of Today's Liturgy

READINGS: Isaiah 22:15, 19–23; Romans 11:33–36;
                Matthew 16:13–20.

REFLECTION

One of the advantages of living so long is that we have more experience and insight to bring to the gospel. How true that is for me in today's reading. Once I saw it almost exclusively as a proof of the primacy of Peter and the indefectibility of the church. Then came a time when I saw it much more personally as a call of Jesus to me to be a disciple. The question to Simon is put to me, "and you, John, or Mary Smith, who do you say I am"? There's no dodging that direct question of faith and the responsibility of discipleship that it implies.

Without dropping the first two insights, I have more recently seen a third level of meaning. Notice when Simon in faith tells Jesus who he is, the messiah, Jesus then tells Simon who he is. He is no longer Simon. He is now the Rock, Peter, and will be such for the rest of his life.

When I give faith or witness to who Jesus is for me, he tells me more about who I am. I'm sure this is what Paul meant in Ephesians when he prayed, "By the power of the Holy Spirit, may you come to know your hidden self." Yes, there's more to each of us and the Spirit of Jesus will respond to our faith in God by revealing more and more about who I really am.

SHARING

How am I progressing in my journey of faith? Is there an image or word or song that expresses where I am right now in my journey?

How do I answer the question of Jesus, "Who do you say that I am"?

As a community how do we help to reveal the hidden self of each other?

How will I help another to uncover a bit of his/her hidden self in my relationships this week?

ACTION RESPONSE

Choose an action that will enable individuals or the group as a whole to live out in the coming week what has been shared.

PRAYER

Allow time for spontaneous prayer and conclude with praying the responsorial psalm of Sunday's liturgy, Psalm 138.

Twenty-Second Sunday of the Year

OPENING PRAYER

The Alternative Opening Prayer of Today's Liturgy

READINGS:
Jeremiah 20:7–9; Romans 12:1–2; Matthew 16:21–27.

REFLECTION

This is another Sunday when the readings are so powerful that it is better to change the procedure and totally let the word read us. Select three people from the group, and let each of those three read slowly aloud the reading. Let there then be a two-minute pause after the reading as each of us ponders that word. Then let the original reader read it again for a second time. After the second reading, let the reader share how the word read intersects with his or her journey. Others then are invited to share. Then move on to the second and third reading and follow the same procedure. So in summary there would be a reading, a pause of two minutes of quiet, a re-reading of the word out loud, and then a sharing of what the word meant to each person in the group.

SHARING

What does the phrase "breaking open the word of God" mean to me?

How will I this week help another to share in the experience of breaking open the word of God?

ACTION RESPONSE

Choose an action that will enable individuals or the group as a whole to live out in the coming week what has been shared.

PRAYER

Allow time for spontaneous prayer and conclude with praying the responsorial psalm of Sunday's liturgy, Psalm 63.

Twenty-Third Sunday of the Year

OPENING PRAYER

The Alternative Opening Prayer of Today's Liturgy

READINGS: Ezekiel 33:7–9; Romans 13:8–10;
                  Matthew 18:15–20.

REFLECTION

Since Vatican II there has been a great revival of the word of God and prayer, and one of the great insights is the return to the deeper pondering within our heart of God's word.

In today's readings there are two powerful one-liners that we need to hear again and at a deeper level. The first is the responsorial psalm, "That today you would hear his voice: Do not harden your hearts." We in the west are in danger of suffering from an excessive head approach to word and to prayer. We need to bring in our heart. The heart in the biblical sense is a whole response. The heart is the point in us where the crossroads of our own history and the movement of God meet. It is there where the word must be resonated and pondered. But unless I am always aware, ever prayerful, my heart will miss God's voice in people, snowflakes, children's laughter, telephone calls, thank-you notes, my own ups and downs—you can add to your own reckoning. But if we have open prayerful hearts, we will hear God's voice and we will hear it today.

The second one-liner is the very last sentence of the gospel, "For where two or three are gathered together in my name, there am I in the midst of them." The miracle of faith is that the power of Jesus' presence is not just adding up numbers, two or three, but when we truly believe that Jesus is present within each and among us, then the total power of presence is more than the sum total of its parts. There is a quantum leap of spiritual power in the special Spirit-presence of Jesus.

SHARING

Where do I most often hear God's voice? Share an example or two.

Have I ever been aware of a special presence of Jesus in community prayer? In what way?

How have our community sharings illuminated either or both of the one-liners of today's scripture?

What concrete action will I take to hear God's voice with my heart?

ACTION RESPONSE

Choose an action that will enable individuals or the group as a whole to live out in the coming week what has been shared.

PRAYER

Allow time for spontaneous prayer and conclude with praying the responsorial psalm of Sunday's liturgy, Psalm 95.

Twenty-Fourth Sunday of the Year

OPENING PRAYER

The Alternative Opening Prayer of Today's Liturgy

READINGS: Sirach 27:30–28:9; Romans 14:7–9;
                  Matthew 18:21–35.

REFLECTION

One of the great benefits of our renewal as a church since Vatican II has been the restoration of our lost legacy of the Old Testament. Each Sunday we hear the word of God before the coming of Christ, illuminating and connecting with the gospel. This week the theme is anger toward my neighbor and the call to forgiveness. Sirach tells it like it really is. "Wrath and anger are hateful things, yet the sinner *hugs* them tight." Should one nourish anger against each other and expect healing from the Lord? I certainly can identify with the hugging of my wounded pride. I won't let go and yet wonder sometimes why there's no healing. What can I say to myself regarding unforgiveness? Hugging it means no healing, and so I must let go if I am to be healed.

Even Peter's question to the Lord is understood better in the context of Jewish numerology. "Lord, if my brother or sister sins against me, how often must I forgive him or her? As many as seven times?" Jesus answered, "I say to you, not seven times but seventy-seven times." It obviously does not mean I become a bookkeeper. It does not mean I wait until the 491 offense to say, "Enough is enough, no more forgiveness." In Jewish terms seventy times seven is a formula for infinite, forever, no end. It has nothing to do with computers. It has everything to do with the intention of the heart. The best time to begin to forgive is not even seven, but one. Otherwise, we waste a lot of time and lose a lot of the freedom of Christ's healing love.

SHARING

Do I maintain a hostile attitude toward anyone? An unforgiving posture? How can I let go of this darkness? Share your response.

Have I ever experienced being forgiven? Can I describe that feeling?

Am I sometimes pragmatic rather than Christian in the command of forgiveness? Give an example.

How have I been healed as a result of letting go of my wounded pride?

As a community do we need to ask or extend forgiveness to anyone in the community or to another person, group or community outside of ourselves? How will we do this?

ACTION RESPONSE

Choose an action that will enable individuals or the group as a whole to live out in the coming week what has been shared.

PRAYER

Allow time for spontaneous prayer and conclude with praying the responsorial psalm of Sunday's liturgy, Psalm 103.

Twenty-Fifth Sunday of the Year

OPENING PRAYER

The Alternative Opening Prayer of Today's Liturgy

READINGS: Isaiah 55:6–9; Philippians 1:20c–24, 27a;
Matthew 20:1–16a.

REFLECTION

If we have any doubts about Isaiah's message, all we have to do is to read the gospel parable. What does Isaiah tell us? "For my thoughts are not your thoughts, nor are your ways my ways, says the Lord."

Isaiah's advice has to be kept in mind when we read the parable. From the human and practical viewpoint, we probably identify with the people who worked all day and thus were upset when they received no more than the late afternoon gang. It's not fair, but again, "My...ways are not your ways." So, too, most Catholics who hear the parable of the prodigal son, identify with the brother who stayed home and worked the farm and would not come out to celebrate the return of his johnny-come-lately brother.

It is the eleventh hour all over again. The Lord is near to all and reads and knows the heart of each of us. The person who is still in the marketplace at a late hour may be the very one wrestling in total honesty with his/her God. Only the Lord knows what struggles are going on in such a person's life. When at last they surrender, it's with a totality that is not measured by length of years, but by quality of response. God patiently waits for the Pauls, the Mary Magdalens, the Augustines. Like Peter, God says to me, "Your business is to follow Me." The Irish used to say, "Mind your own business" and leave the mystery of the reign of God to the providence of God. "My…ways are not your ways."

SHARING

Have I personally experienced God's way not being mine at times? Share your response.

Do I waste a lot of time and effort in not seeking the reign of God myself, and rather resenting special favors shown to others? Give an example.

What is an example that helps us see that, "The last will be first and the first will be last"?

How am I willing to choose to "be last" this week?

ACTION RESPONSE

Choose an action that will enable individuals or the group as a whole to live out in the coming week what has been shared.

PRAYER

Allow time for spontaneous prayer and conclude with praying the responsorial psalm of Sunday's liturgy, Psalm 145.

Twenty-Sixth Sunday of the Year

OPENING PRAYER

The Alternative Opening Prayer of Today's Liturgy

READINGS: Ezekiel 18:25–28; Philippians 2:1–11 or 2:1–5;
                  Matthew 21:28–32.

REFLECTION

This Sunday's readings continue the mystery of God's grace and point out reasons ("dodges") that we present which distract us in our pursuit of the reign of God.

The first dodge of Ezekiel is, "The Lord's way is not fair!" So, like pouting children, we often are angry at God because we decide God is unjust, but Ezekiel counters this with the head-on argument of the Lord. "When a virtuous person turns away from virtue to commit iniquity, and dies, it is because of the iniquity he committed that he must die. But if a wicked person, turning from the wickedness he has committed, does what is right and just, he shall preserve his life."

The gospel tells us not to be taken in by words alone. Look to the action. One son says "yes" to service for his father, but never goes into the field. The second says "no," but regrets it and goes out and works. Who really does the will of the father?

Lastly, Jesus warns us that our justice is a matter of conversion. Don't be taken in by the nice people who do nothing with regard to God's call. They're too comfortable to change. Often times the wrong people, like the prostitutes, can and did in Jesus' time respond with generosity.

So there are many dodges to avoid the decision of repentance or conversion. "God's not fair." "Yes, but later." "What, join those terrible people?" We can easily make a cult of being "the artful dodger."

SHARING

Have I ever grumbled "no" to the Lord and eventually said "yes" in what I did? Share your response.

In what instances have I failed to pursue a movement of God because the wrong people were already involved in that movement?

As a community how have we been guilty of dodging important needs outside of our community?

What needs might we respond to this week?

ACTION RESPONSE

Choose an action that will enable individuals or the group as a whole to live out in the coming week what has been shared.

PRAYER

Allow time for spontaneous prayer and conclude with praying the responsorial psalm of Sunday's liturgy, Psalm 125:1–9.

Twenty-Seventh Sunday of the Year

OPENING PRAYER

The Alternative Opening Prayer of Today's Liturgy

READINGS: Isaiah 5:1–7; Philippians 4:6–9;
Matthew 21:33–43.

REFLECTION

The image of the vineyard runs through the readings from Isaiah, the psalm and the gospel, and the Lord lets there be no doubt as to who is symbolized by the vineyard. "The vineyard of the Lord of hosts is the house of Israel." A very comfortable interpretation for me as a Christian is to say, that the Israelites did not tend the vineyard so the Lord gave it to another nation "that will yield a rich harvest," and this, of course, is the Christian community. Have we as a people and I as a disciple tended the vineyard well and yielded a rich harvest?

There is a tendency in all of us to tone down God's justice. We say it is something in the old order and has given way to the new Christian dispensation of love. God is simple, and God's love and justice are both bonded in the divine balance.

It might be well if we allowed the full word of Isaiah and Matthew to be interiorized by ourselves as disciples and as part of a community. Can I honestly say that I am innocent of the accusation of the Lord? Perhaps then we can say with the psalmist:

"Attend to this vine
Then we will not withdraw from you;
Revive us and we will call on your name."

SHARING

How do I answer the Lord's question, "What more was there to do for my vineyard that I had not done"?

Have I ever experienced the peace of Paul in the first paragraph of Philippians? Share those experiences.

What has been our greatest failure in neglecting some portion of the vineyard of the world?

How can we respond to the needs that we have neglected?

ACTION RESPONSE

Choose an action that will enable individuals or the group as a whole to live out in the coming week what has been shared.

PRAYER

Allow time for spontaneous prayer and conclude with praying the responsorial psalm of Sunday's liturgy, Psalm 80.

Twenty-Eighth Sunday of the Year

OPENING PRAYER

The Alternative Opening Prayer of Today's Liturgy

READINGS: Isaiah 25:6–10a; Philippians 4:12–14, 19–20;
Matthew 22:1–14 or 22:1–10.

REFLECTION

Once again we have a very rich image that runs like a delicate thread through all four readings. Isaiah speaks of the rich feast of food and wine on the Lord's day; the psalmist sees the Good Shepherd as spreading a table before us; Paul knows both how to eat well and go hungry; Matthew tells the story of the king who invites all kinds of people to a wedding banquet.

So many of our own personal images are evoked. Our happiest memory, perhaps, is of a warm table at home where we celebrated life and laughter at a family meal. We may long for it today, but it is rare that a family has the time or desire to break in a leisurely fashion. Our age suffers from fast food services which are automated and impersonal. We long for the shared table.

Another image that is not too happy is the memory of being sent from the table for our young foibles. It, too, is a symbol of our alienated and lonely age. More often than not we exclude ourselves from the banquet when we refuse to be garbed in the desire for God's grace. At times our pride drowns out the gentle invitation of the Lord to come in and break bread with us. And yet God's invitation is insistent. "Behold, I stand at the door and knock. If anyone opens, I will come in and share with his meal."

SHARING

What images speak loudest to me from the twenty-third psalm, images that connect with my own experience?

How do I relate to Paul's experience in Philippians?

As a community do we break bread together and how are we concerned about the lack of bread among the needy people of our world? What will we do?

ACTION RESPONSE

Choose an action that will enable individuals or the group as a whole to live out in the coming week what has been shared.

PRAYER

Allow time for spontaneous prayer and conclude with praying the responsorial psalm of Sunday's liturgy, Psalm 23.

Twenty-Ninth Sunday of the Year

OPENING PRAYER

The Alternative Opening Prayer of Today's Liturgy

READINGS: Isaiah 45:1, 4–6; 1 Thessalonians 1:1–5b;
                  Matthew 22:15–21.

REFLECTION

Some years ago Jacques Maritain entitled one of his books, *The Things that Are Not Caesar's*; and those things belong to God alone. One of the areas that belongs to the Lord is a quality portion of our time, for as Rahner says, "The only stringless gift I can give to another is my time; for when I give you my time, I give a portion of my life that will never return."

A good barometer of a quality time that I give to God is the measure of my prayer for it is in prayer that I hear God "call me by name" (Isaiah). "It is in prayer that I can thank God for all my companions and remember them" (Paul). The experience of prayer helps me to discern the spirit of God, and like Jesus, prayer will give me a wisdom not to be trapped and a strength to implement my prayerful vision (Matthew). Since Vatican II we have been more sensitive to the concept of the reign of God cutting across all life and history. It is a God whose reign is found in the things and time and eternity of spirit and of matter. It includes even the things of Caesar, but without reflective prayer we will miss the revelation of God in the material and temporal realm of Caesar. Once more we have to avoid the either/or mentality. Prayer will help us to become a both/and people.

SHARING

What quality time do I give to God in prayer? Be honest and specific.

How do I sometimes fall into the trap of over-spiritualizing my prayer, making it a cop-out from life?

How are we doing in community in our shared prayer?

How does my prayer affect my decisions and actions in the broader community of the church?

Think about a concrete decision you need to make this week. What kind of prayer commitment will you make in order to gain wisdom for the decision?

ACTION RESPONSE

Choose an action that will enable individuals or the group as a whole to live out in the coming week what has been shared.

PRAYER

Allow time for spontaneous prayer and conclude with praying the responsorial psalm of Sunday's liturgy, Psalm 96.

Thirtieth Sunday of the Year

OPENING PRAYER

The Alternative Opening Prayer of Today's Liturgy

READINGS: Exodus 22:20–26; 1 Thessalonians 1:5c–10;
Matthew 22:34–40.

REFLECTION

In the Sunday readings of last week, we heard the enemies of Jesus try to trap him in his speech. In this week's readings a lawyer tries to trip him up. Jesus uses the same argument that is reflected in all this week's readings, namely, experience. He replies to the lawyer on his own ground. He quotes the scripture of the religious constitution of the Israelites, the love of God and neighbor and self which one has to experience to be considered a Jew.

The experience of what once-we-were must never be forgotten and shapes our attitude to others. As Exodus tells the Jews not to oppress an alien, "for you were once aliens yourselves in the land of Egypt." The psalmist's love of God is based on his experience of God as "my rock, my fortress, my deliverer." Again, Paul, in his relation to the Thessalonians, lauds them because they have experienced receiving the word "with joy from the Holy Spirit," and they can go on to become a model of faith for others because the word has "sounded forth." Only the God whom we truly experience in our life, our prayer, our ministry, and word has power to free us from being "trapped" or "tripped up."

SHARING

Is there a person in your life who by his/her actions reveals that he/she has received the word "with joy from the Holy Spirit"?

Can you recall a specific instance in your life when you experienced God as your rock?—your fortress?—your deliverer?

How have I experienced God in my journey in the last month? Be specific.

Like the Thessalonians, how have we as a community modeled Christ to the parish and/or the broader community?

How can we grow in love in our broader community?

ACTION RESPONSE

Choose an action that will enable individuals or the group as a whole to live out in the coming week what has been shared.

PRAYER

Allow time for spontaneous prayer and conclude with praying the responsorial psalm of Sunday's liturgy, Psalm 18.

Thirty-First Sunday of the Year

OPENING PRAYER

The Alternative Opening Prayer of Today's Liturgy

READINGS: Malachi 1:14b—2:2b, 8–10; 1 Thessalonians
2:7b–9, 13; Matthew 23:1–12.

REFLECTION

The theme in today's readings is that our lives touch one another deeply. It is for this reason that the prophet confronts us with the question, "Why then do we break faith with each other"? Because our lives act as models for one another, Jesus tells his contemporaries to do anything the Pharisees teach, "but do not follow their example." Perhaps the most graphic exhortation falling from the truth of people's touching people is found in Paul. He so loves the Thessalonians that he is willing to share not only the good news, "but our very lives as well, so dearly beloved had you become to us."

Isn't this what Jesus means when he calls us to serve one another, sharing not just things we do, but sharing the heart of who we are? It gets to the real nitty-gritty of love; loving myself in my neighbor and my neighbor in myself. Only in authentic self-love can I become an instrument of sharing my life with another for that is how all of us are touched by one another. We are people who need people.

SHARING

How have I been touched by another in some significant point of my journey?

Have I ever been told by another that I touched them? Share the experience.

How will I touch the world and make a difference?

What specific action will I do this week to share with another the heart of who I am?

ACTION RESPONSE

Choose an action that will enable individuals or the group as a whole to live out in the coming week what has been shared.

PRAYER

Allow time for spontaneous prayer and conclude with praying the responsorial psalm of Sunday's liturgy, Psalm 131.

Thirty-Second Sunday of the Year

OPENING PRAYER

The Alternative Opening Prayer of Today's Liturgy

READINGS: Wisdom 6:12–16; 1 Thessalonians 4:13–18 or 4:13–14; Matthew 25:1–13.

REFLECTION

"Keep your eyes open, for you know not the day or the hour." This used to be a standard text of retreat and mission preachers trying to frighten us into being good. Not only does it do violence to the biblical meaning, but it is contrary to our own experience. Recall a long absence of a dear friend. Then one day on a dreary, rainy morning you throw the door open and there stands the friend, coming unexpectedly as an ambassador of joy and surprise. So, too, should the coming of the Lord be, a Lord of surprise, of joy and fulfillment.

The readings call upon us to cooperate with the Lord's coming by awareness, desire and hunger for God. Wisdom, we are told, "is readily perceived by those who love her, and found by those who seek her." The wise virgins provide for the unexpected return of the beloved. The psalmist most poignantly describes his thirst for the Lord and compares his being to the earth, parched and lifeless without the water of God's presence.

As always, the difficult tradition calls upon us to be responsible and alert in seeking the Lord. The opening prayer of the liturgy captures it beautifully, "Help us to become more aware of your loving design so that we may more willingly open our lives in service to all."

SHARING

How has God found me in my seeking?

Do I see a connection between prayer and awareness? In what way?

How well do we as a small group/community connect the prayer of the liturgy's "awareness to your design" and "giving our lives in service" to the broader community around us?

This week, what will I do specifically to connect prayer and service?

ACTION RESPONSE

Choose an action that will enable individuals or the group as a whole to live out in the coming week what has been shared.

PRAYER

Allow time for spontaneous prayer and conclude with praying the responsorial psalm of Sunday's liturgy, Psalm 63.

Thirty-Third Sunday of the Year

OPENING PRAYER

The Alternative Opening Prayer of Today's Liturgy

READINGS: Proverbs 31:10–13, 19–20, 30–31; 1 Thessalonians
5:1–6; Matthew 25:14–30 or 25:14–15, 19–20.

REFLECTION

In the gospel story today the person going away entrusted gifts to
three stewards "according to each person's abilities." Two developed the
gifts, but a third, out of fear, buried it. The master praised those who
developed in trust the gifts that were given and scolded and then took
away the gift of the one who buried it. Then the moral of the story, "For
to everyone who has, more will be given and they will grow rich; but
from the one who has not, even what the person has will be taken away."

The key words are trust and risk. If I open my life and am
vulnerable and risk and share my love, joy or knowledge, I will grow in
love, joy and wisdom. But out of a false security if I close up and protect
my gift and bury it, not only will I not save it, but my love, joy or
knowledge will atrophy or dry up. In the language of the day I will go
down the tubes on the installment plan.

To be a Christian one is called to risk and trust, to be willing to be
vulnerable as is Christ. We are called by the gospel to scatter, not hoard.
The Sea of Galilee and the Dead Sea are symbols of our very selves.
Galilee's sea is open and gives and is alive, teeming with fish. The other
sea in the south is landlocked, turns in on itself, is lifeless, is called the
Dead Sea.

SHARING

How have I grown in giving to another in trust?

Have there ever been moments in my own life when out of fear I declined to grow?

As a community are we inclined to be more open to each other or afraid? Give some examples.

What makes me fearful? What specific actions will I do this week to change fear into trust?

ACTION RESPONSE

Choose an action that will enable individuals or the group as a whole to live out in the coming week what has been shared.

PRAYER

Allow time for spontaneous prayer and conclude with praying the responsorial psalm of Sunday's liturgy, Psalm 128.

Thirty-Fourth or Last Sunday of the Year (Christ the King)

OPENING PRAYER

The Alternative Opening Prayer of Today's Liturgy

READINGS: Ezekiel 34:11–12, 15–17; 1 Corinthians 15:20–26, 28; Matthew 25:31–46.

REFLECTION

The liturgical year ends with a proclamation of the kind of kingdom we believe in and the kind of relationship we have with our king, Christ. It is not an abstract but a highly personal relationship.

Ezekiel tells us that "The Lord himself will shepherd his people." Hear what he has to say: "*I* myself will look after and tend. The lost *I* will seek out, the strayed *I* will bring back. The injured *I* will bind up, the sick *I* will heal."

In the New Testament the bottom line of all life and living in the reign of God is that the communal dimension is identified with the personal and at end time Jesus sees no disparity between himself and all his brothers and sisters. "I was hungry…naked…a stranger…What you did not do for one of these least ones, you did not do for me."

Our relationship is at once a highly personal one with Jesus. It is also identified with Jesus in his and our brothers and sisters. There is a danger of making it a "me and Jesus" relationship or just "doing good for others." Our relationship with Jesus our king is wed in a love of the individual and community.

SHARING

How would I describe my personal relationship with the Lord at this point in time?

How have I experienced knowing Christ in the stranger, the needy, the homeless?

How do I in my family, neighborhood, workplace balance individual and communal needs around me?

What will I do this week to bring greater balance of individual and community relationships into focus?

ACTION RESPONSE

Choose an action that will enable individuals or the group as a whole to live out in the coming week what has been shared.

PRAYER

Allow time for spontaneous prayer and conclude with praying the responsorial psalm of Sunday's liturgy, Psalm 23.

Prayer Resources

(All prayers in this section were written by RENEW staff and volunteers except where noted.)

ADVENT/CHRISTMAS SEASON

O Light of the nations, shed your
brilliance upon our troubled
world. Light up our minds to see
clearly how to live justly and
peacefully. Help us to bring your
light to people in darkness that
we may be one world under your
loving reign. Amen.

O Emmanuel, we watch and wait
for your coming anew into our
hearts and into our world. Give
us insight and patience as we
wait. Do not delay. Help us not
to miss your many
manifestations. Amen.

Tender God, prepare and tame our
wild hearts. Make level the
rough places in our hearts so
that we can more easily
recognize your coming. You
promised through Isaiah that
your glory would be revealed and

that all people would see your
glory together. Grace us with
your glory once again. We ask
this in Jesus' name. Amen.

Lord, God of power and might,
you are Lord of darkness and
light. When we lose our way and
stumble through dark moments
be by our side. When the
brilliance of your light shines
forth let our hearts be grateful.
We sing our Hosannas for our
Savior has come and all of
heaven and earth is full of God's
glory. Amen.

LENTEN/EASTER SEASON

Jesus, risen Lord, thank you for
showing us how to live our
dreams and hopes as you did.
Thank you for teaching us to
believe in the mystery and power
of God, that wonderful life-
giving God that raised you to
new life and promises us the
same new life. Amen.

We sing our "Alleluia," Lord
Jesus, as we gather in your light.
You restored sight to the blind
and made the deaf hear. May the
steady flame of your passionate
love for us kindle our spirits so
that our "Alleluias" may always
well up within us and resound
throughout the world. Amen.

To the Paschal Victim (Easter)
Christians, to the Paschal Victim
Offer your thankful praises!
A Lamb the sheep redeems:
Christ, who only is sinless,
Reconciles sinners to the Father.
Death and life have contended in
that combat stupendous:
The Prince of life, who died,
reigns immortal.
Speak, Mary, declaring
What you saw, wayfaring.
"The tomb of Christ, who is living,
The glory of Jesus' resurrection;
Bright angels attesting,
The shroud and napkin resting.
Yes, Christ my hope is arisen: To
Galilee he goes before you."
Christ indeed from death is risen,
our new life obtaining.
Have mercy, victor King, ever
reigning! Amen. Alleluia
(Taken from *Lectionary for Mass*,
Catholic Book Publishing Co.,
New York, 1970.)

Jesus, through your resurrection,
you brought great hope to Mary
and to your disciples. Open our
eyes to your presence in those
we meet today. May we be a
hope-filled people who live in
integrity and justice. Amen.

Praise be to you Creator God.
You have given us new birth, a
new hope by raising Jesus from
the dead. May our lives be filled
with the promise of eternal joy.

As we strive to live fully the joy
of your resurrection, help us to
die to ourselves, like the grain
of wheat, so that we, too, may
live, and bear fruit in
abundance. Amen.

Spirit of the Lord, rest upon us
and move us to bring good news
to the poor and oppressed. Help
us too, to be in touch with our
own poverty. We have been
called to be for one another.
Bring to birth within us the light
of truth and the burning gift of
God's love. Amen.

Holy Spirit, you come upon Mary
and the apostles gathered in fear
in the upper room. Calm our
fears and our troubled hearts.
Help us to believe in your gentle
presence among us. Empower us
to be Jesus' disciples without
counting the cost. Amen.

Mary, the Evangelist
O Mary, you were the first
Christian evangelist. By God's
invitation through the angel
Gabriel and by your free choice
you accepted Jesus into your life.
By giving birth to Jesus you gifted
us with our most wonderful
brother and friend and savior.
Thank you, Mary, for being with
the apostles when you welcomed
the Holy Spirit who empowered all
of you to evangelize the world.

Pray that the same Holy Spirit
will empower us today to be good
evangelizers. Be our mother and
mediatrix today, Mary. Amen.

Pentecost Sequence
Come, Holy Spirit, come!
And from your celestial home
    Shed a ray of light divine!
Come, Father of the poor!
Come, source of all our store!
    Come, within our bosoms shine!
You, of comforters the best;
You, the soul's most welcome
guest;
    Sweet refreshment here below;
In our labor, rest most sweet;
Grateful coolness in the heat;
    Solace in the midst of woe.
O most blessed Light divine,
Shine within these hearts of yours,
    And our inmost being fill!
Where you are not, people have naught,
Nothing good in deed or thought,
    Nothing free from taint of ill.
Heal our wounds, our strength renew;
On our dryness pour your dew;
    Wash the stains of guilt away:
Bend the stubborn heart and will;
Melt the frozen, warm the chill;
    Guide the steps that go astray.
On the faithful, who adore
And confess you, evermore
    In your sev'nfold gift descend;
Give them virtue's sure reward;
Give them your salvation, Lord;
    Give them joys that never end.
Amen. Alleluia.
(Adapted from *Lectionary for Mass,*

Catholic Book Publishing Co.,
New York, 1970.)

ORDINARY TIME

O Gracious God, you never leave
our presence. Help us to take
time to recognize you in our
midst and to give thanks for all
your goodness to us. Teach us to
love you more and more each
day. Amen.

Gentle God, sometimes we are so
hard on ourselves. Help us to see
ourselves and others as you see
us—made in your image and
likeness. Create in us great joy
to celebrate your many faces! Amen.

Forgiving God, you show us in so
many ways, especially through
the sacraments, that you want
us to live in your forgiving love.
Give us joy and peace to serve
you and our sisters and brothers
in genuine freedom. Amen.

Our souls will know your peace,
O Lord, and our weary hearts
need only surrender to your will.
It is then, Lord, that you can
teach us where true glory reigns.
Give to us, O Lord, your Spirit so
we may know that what we seek
waits quietly within our
hearts. Amen.

Dear God, thank you for bringing
us together again. Let us relish

your presence among us so that
our hearts may be filled with
love. We depend upon you for
everything and place ourselves
in your care now and always. Amen.

God of our being, you have loved
us into life. All we are and have
is from you. Keep us always
mindful of our dependence upon
you. During our time together give
us new insight into what trusting
and depending on you really means.
We ask this through Jesus our
brother. Amen.

Gentle, loving God, in you we
place the deepest desires of our
hearts. You have formed us in
the deep recesses of your own
heart. Let this time of prayer be
a union of our hearts with the
divine heart of your son, Jesus. Amen.

Source of all truth, open our
minds and hearts to seek truth
all our days. Give us courage to
speak your truth gently and
lovingly whenever you prompt us.
And help us to be open to receive
the truth from others. Amen.

Lord God, how good it is to be
alive this day. May we live each
moment aware of your goodness
and love. Help us to be a source
of your love to those we meet
along the way. Amen.

My soul, O Lord, longs to hear
your word. Speak to us the word

that will both comfort and
challenge us. Ignite in our
hearts the gift of compassion to
accompany us along life's path.
Sear deeply our whole being so
that we may take the risks that
enables your promises to be
fulfilled. Amen.

O God, the words, "the Lord sets
captives free" assure us that you
are faithful to all people. May
we respond to the call to be
Christ to others as we give food
to the hungry, secure justice for
the oppressed and help to set
captives free. We ask, too, Lord
that you give sight to our
blindness and support us when
we feel low and bowed down.
Come Lord and save us! Amen.

Jesus, you are very near to all.
May we trust in your promise as
we stumble along our way. Let
us touch your outstretched hand
and feel deeply your tender love. Amen.

Creator God you formed us out of
love to be love. May our journey
on this earth lead us through the
events of life that call forth our
unconditional love for others. Amen.

Our hearts are weary, Lord, for
we are broken and afraid. Quiet
and still these anxious hearts
and protect us from all harm.
Give to us the serenity that is

yours so that our restless
spirits may be comforted, for we
truly know that the peace we
seek is already within us. Amen.

O God, you are both Mother and
Father to us. We are the clay,
you are the potter. Mold us and
fashion us as you will for we
desire to be open to your design
for us. Amen.

RENEW Prayer to Mary

Mary, you are a woman
wrapped in silence
and yet the Word
born of your yes
continues to bring life
to all creation.
Mary, help us to say yes—
to be bearers of good news
to a world waiting.

Mary, you are a virgin
and a mother
empowered by the Holy Spirit.
Help us to open ourselves
to that same life-bringing Spirit.
Mary, help us to say our yes.

Mary, you are gift of Jesus to us,
mother of the church.
Look upon our world
and our lives.
Pray for us to your Son
that we might be renewed
that we might help renew
the face of the earth.
Mary, help us to say yes. Amen.

The Memorare
Remember, O most gracious Virgin
Mary, that never was it known
that anyone who fled to your
protection, implored your help, or
sought your intercession, was left
unaided. Inspired by this
confidence, I fly unto you, O virgin
of virgins, my Mother. To you I
come; before you I stand sinful
and sorrowful. O Mother of the
Word Incarnate! Despise not my
petitions, but in your mercy hear
and answer me. Amen. (St. Bernard)

Prayer of St. Francis of Assisi
Lord, make me an instrument
of your peace:
where there is hatred, let me sow love;
where there is injury, pardon;
where there is doubt, faith;
where there is despair, hope;
where there is darkness, light;
and where there is sadness, joy.
O, Divine Master, grant that I may not so much seek
to be consoled as to console,
to be understood as to understand,
to be loved as to love.
For it is in giving that we receive,
it is in pardoning that we are pardoned,
and it is in dying that we are born
to eternal life. Amen.
(Attributed to Francis of Assisi)

Prayer for Renew
LORD, We are your people,
    the sheep of your flock.
Heal the sheep who are wounded,
Touch the sheep who are in pain,

Clean the sheep who are soiled,
Warm the lambs who are cold.

Help us to know the Father's love
　　through Jesus the shepherd
　　and through the Spirit.
Help us to lift up that love,
　　and show it all over this land.
Help us to build love on justice
　　and justice on love.
Help us to believe mightily,
　　hope joyfully,
　　love divinely.

Renew us that we may help renew
　　the face of the earth. Amen.

Prayer Dream

Our Father, Unseen God in the heavens—
　　You are holy, kind and wonderful…!
How we wish for your loving plan to become
　　as real on our earth as it is in heaven:
　　For then
All will be healthy and fed
　　in body and in spirit;
All will be happy and satisfied.
　　For everyone is your child,
　　a daughter or a son,
　　precious and loved.
Help us to live together in peace,
　　forgiving each other's
mistakes,
just as you hold nothing against
us, ever.
And then we will have heaven on
our earth. Amen. (Emery Tang, OFM)

Apostles' Creed

I believe in God, the Father
almighty, Creator of heaven and

earth; and in Jesus Christ, his
only Son, our Lord, who was
conceived by the Holy Spirit,
born of the Virgin Mary, suffered
under Pontius Pilate, was
crucified, died, and was buried.
He descended into hell;
the third day he rose again from the dead;
he ascended into heaven,
sitteth at the right hand of God,
the Father almighty, from thence
he shall come to judge the living
and the dead.
I believe in the Holy Spirit,
the holy Catholic Church,
the communion of saints,
the forgiveness of sins,
the resurrection of the body,
and life everlasting. Amen.

Glory to God

Glory to God in the highest,
　　and peace to all people on earth.
Lord God, heavenly King,
almighty God and Father,
　　we worship you, we give
　　you thanks, we praise you
　　for your glory.
Lord Jesus Christ,
only Son of the Father,
Lord God, Lamb of God,
you take away the sin of the
world:
　　have mercy on us;
you are seated at the right hand
of the Father:
　　receive our prayer.
For you alone are the Holy One,
you alone are the Lord,

you alone are the Most High,
Jesus Christ,
with the Holy Spirit,
in the glory of God the Father. Amen.

Suggested Action Responses

The most effective actions are usually not projects separate from everyday life but the integration of our Christian conviction in our family life, work, recreation and places of activity. Therefore, the most appropriate action is usually one very unique to the individual that is connected with the circumstances and challenges of everyday life. Changing the environment or society in which we live is probably the most valuable way of putting faith in practice.

When this type of action step is not immediately evident it is worth considering projects that are connected with our sharing and may be particularly timely. The following suggestions are not intended to limit imagination but to aid creativity especially when the action response is aimed toward a project.

Visit elderly, shut-ins, prisoners, sick.

Provide transportation to elderly and disabled for doctor's visits, grocery shopping, community activities, church.

Organize people to come together to work on community problems (i.e., drugs, crime, unsafe neighborhoods).

Provide cultural activities for disadvantaged youth.

Stock food banks and provide food baskets.

Become involved in organizations such as Bread for the World, Habitat for Humanity, Amnesty International, Pax Christi.

Start a food co-op in your area.

Work with youth groups to organize a neighborhood or community clean-up project.

Work in soup kitchens.

Protest to advertisers or television stations regarding the following: violence, sexual promiscuity, vulgar language, inappropriate role models for children and teenagers, and making fun of those who oppose cruelty to animals.

Plant a vegetable garden and share some of your harvest with others in need.

Provide clothing to clothing centers.

Work ecumenically to open food banks and soup kitchens.

Assist with Meals on Wheels to be effective in the local area.

Staff emergency assistance centers.

Assist at homeless shelters.

Set up shelters for the homeless or provide parish resources for housing the homeless.

Educate children about our dependence on each other and on the natural world.

Paint homes for disadvantaged people.

Recycle bottles, cans, plastic, paper, clothes.

Work with municipal and state authorities to implement recycling programs or centers.

Provide furniture for those in need.

Visit nursing homes and provide needed care and support.

Host rummage sales where profits are used for the needy.

Gather baby clothes for young pregnant teens or teen moms.

Buy recycled products; reuse grocery bags.

Share with and support terminally ill people.

Clean-up campaigns for neighborhood parks.

Sponsor ecumenical social activities to bring people together to celebrate special occasions.

Join community-based groups that work to conserve resources, to save and protect the environment.

Have a simple vegetarian meal once a week; donate your savings to an appropriate cause.

Help with literacy needs in the community.

Tutor those with special educational needs.

Help with voter registration.

Write a letter to a prisoner or someone in a hospital or nursing home.

Write letters to leaders in Congress regarding concerns for the poor and disadvantaged or to address community needs (i.e., housing needs).

Take a nature walk and reflect on your connectedness with all of creation.

Organize neighborhoods for community improvements addressing total community needs, particularly neighborhood housing needs.

Save energy: insulate adequately your home; turn off lights and appliances when appropriate.

Do without unnecessary appliances, e.g., electric can-openers, knives, etc.

Attend a local city government and school board meeting and encourage community values.

Walk, bicycle, car pool, use public transportation.

Be a voice for the poor and homeless at community meetings.

Try to live more simply so resources can be distributed more equally.

Be a voice for the poor and homeless at community meetings.

Try to live more simply so resources can be distributed more equally.